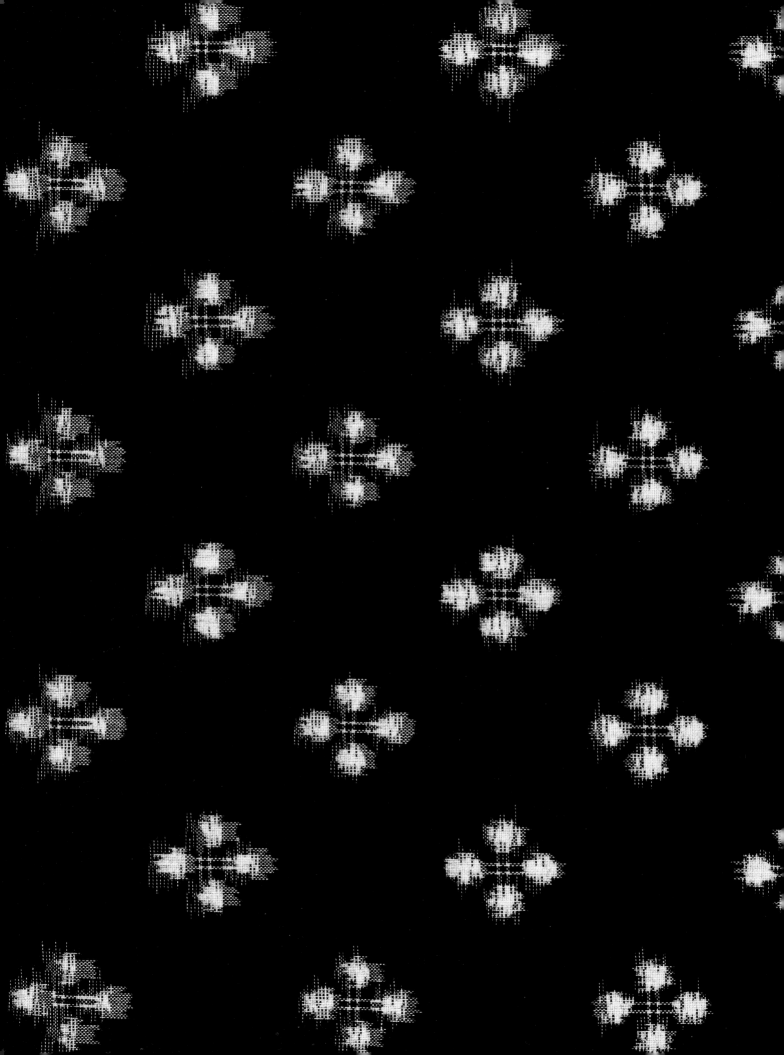

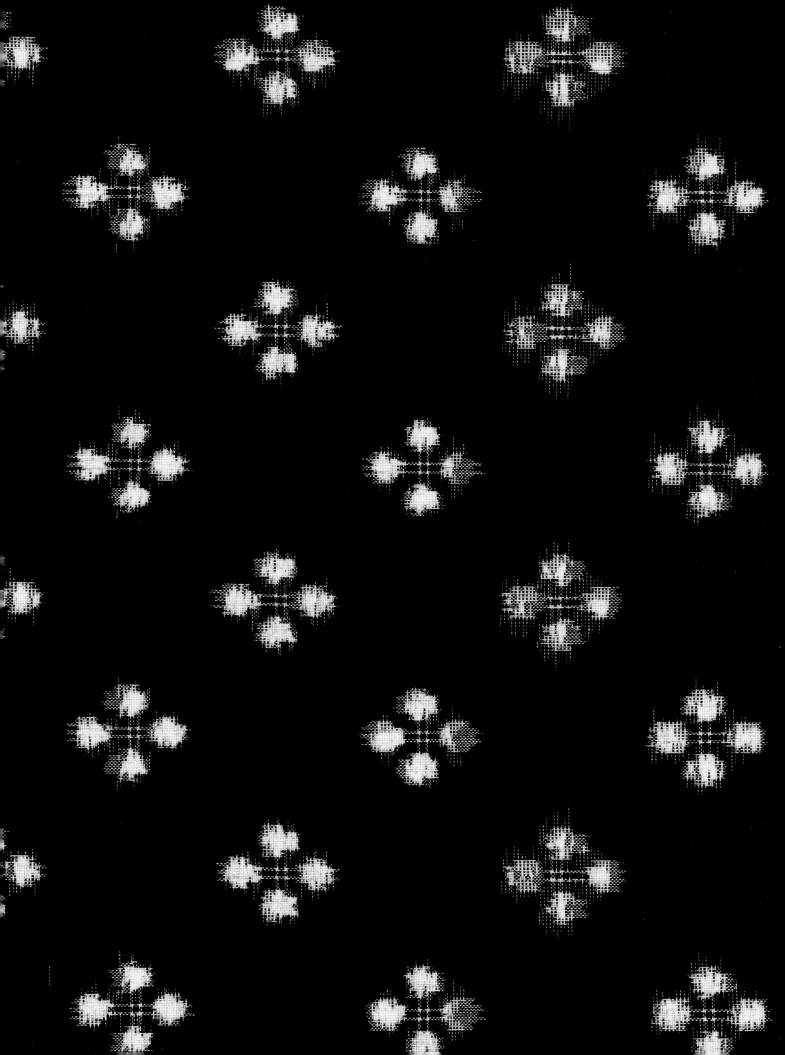

EAST
QUILTS
WEST

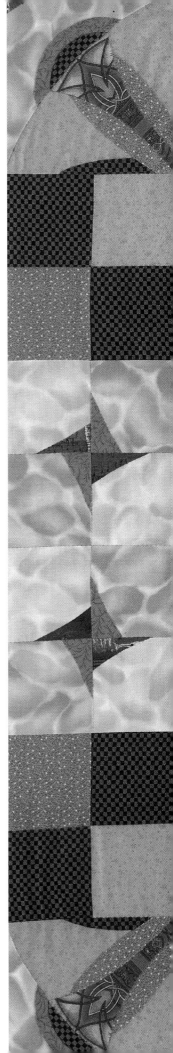

東キルト西二

KUMIKO SUDO

EAST
QUILTS
WEST
II

 THE QUILT DIGEST PRESS
Simply the Best from NTC Publishing Group

Editing by Nancy Bruning.
Technical editing and assembly diagrams by Kandy Petersen.
Block diagrams and templates by Green Lizard Design, St. Helena.
Copyediting by Janet Reed.
Cover design by Kajun Graphics, San Francisco.
Book design by Rick Dinihanian & John Lyle, Green Lizard Design, St. Helena.
Quilt photography by Sharon Risedorph, San Francisco.

Printed in Hong Kong.

The author thanks Hoffman California Fabrics, Momen House Fabrics, P&B
Textiles, Peter Pan Fabric, RJR Fashion Fabrics, VIP, and Clover Needlecraft, Inc.,
for their support.

First printing

Library of Congress Cataloging-in-Publication Data
(Revised for volume 2)

Sudo, Kumiko.
  East quilts West.

  Vol. 2 has edition statement: 1st ed.
  1. Sudo, Kumiko—Themes, motives. 2. Quilts—Japan—
History—20th century. 3. Quilts—United States—
History—20th century. 4. Quilting—Patterns. I. Title.
NK9198.S8A4 1992   746.3'92   92-24027
ISBN 0-913327-37-9 (v. 1) Now published under 0-8442-2637-8
ISBN 0-913327-47-6 (v. 2) Published under 0-8442-2643-2

Published by The Quilt Digest Press,
a division of NTC Publishing Group
4255 West Touhy Avenue,
Lincolnwood (Chicago), Illinois 60646-1975 U.S.A.

5 6 7 8 9 WKT 9 8 7 6 5 4 3 2 1

人はいさ
心もしらず
ふるさとは
花ぞむかしの
香ににほひける
小倉百人一首
紀貫之

This poem tells the story of a nobleman, Kino Tsurayuki, who during
the Heian period made a trip back to his hometown on New Year's day.
His lover lived in this town, and he wanted to visit her on his way to
the temple. Arriving at her home, he discovered that she had gone, but
in her garden was a lovely plum tree in full bloom with a sweet
fragrance to greet him. As he stood there broken hearted, he began
thinking about life and compared the inconsistency of human beings
with the faithfulness of nature's annual beauty.

CONTENTS

8 *Introduction: A Walk in Kumiko Sudo's Fabric Flower Garden*

16 *How to Use This Book*

21 *Blocks and Quilts*

22 CAMELLIA

23 PRIMROSE

24 MAGNOLIA

25 FUCHSIA ✿

30 THISTLE

31 CROWN IMPERIAL

32 COCKSCOMB

33 CHINESE LANTERN

34 HONEYSUCKLE

35 EGYPTIAN LOTUS ✿

40 CORNFLOWER

41 FLAME TREE

42 DAFFODIL

43 CALLA LILY ✿

48 LILY OF THE VALLEY

49 PEONY

50 FRENCH LAVENDER

51 HOLLYHOCK

52 PARROT'S BEAK

53 SHAMROCK ✿

58 MANDEVILLA

59 MAGIC FLOWER OF THE INCAS

60 GOLDEN COIN

61 ANGEL TRUMPET ✿

66 CYCLAMEN

67 GLADIOLUS

68 ROSE

69 EVERGREEN MAGNOLIA

70 IRIS

71 CHERRY BLOSSOM ✿

77 *Templates*

125 *Lesson Plans*

✿ *Instructions for full quilts follow these block pages.*

INTRODUCTION

*A Walk in Kumiko Sudo's
Fabric Flower Garden*

Kumiko Sudo's choice to use flowers as her theme for this book is a logical outgrowth of her previous work and her Japanese heritage. Traditional Japanese design is steeped in images from the natural world, reflecting an age-old sensitivity to the environment. Kumiko explains, "We all have a need to create beauty within ourselves and share with others in the same dream. Since we all like to spend some time in a flower garden, I asked myself, Why not grow my own hybrid flowers with fabrics?" In the following conversation with Kumiko Sudo, she elaborates on this new design direction and explores the deeper significance of flowers in her life and in all our lives.

What are the sources of your inspiration and design ability?

I draw design inspiration from my everyday life, my culture, my present, and my past. My early interest in fabrics, shapes, and color stems in part from my father, who was a professional photographer. Since color film was not yet available, he would often brush pigments on the individual photographs. He invented his own techniques and would cut shapes, such as flowers, from paper and incorporate them into the photographs. My mother influenced me as well. She and I each kept pictorial journals. Hers were full of collages of flowers and fruits, and even cows with wreaths around their necks. My mother was also an instructor in flower arrangement and a good dressmaker and knitter who created her own designs. I became involved in her dressmaking business and then was introduced to fine art. I traveled

▲ THIS KIMONO HAS BLUE AND CREAM COLORS THAT FADE TO AND FROM EACH OTHER. IN JAPAN THIS TECHNIQUE IS CALLED *BOKASHI*. THE FLOWER DESIGN IS FROM THE TANGERINE TREE, WHICH IN JAPANESE IS CALLED *TACHIBANA*.

▶ (FACING PAGE) MY FATHER'S FAVORITE HOBBY WAS THAT OF BONSAI. HE TOOK CARE OF MANY BONSAI PLANTS, AND THIS PARTICULAR PINE TREE WAS ONE OF HIS MOST UNUSUAL.

all over the world, visiting museums, and when I encountered antique quilts in Palo Alto, California, I knew I had finally found my life work.

What is the significance of flowers and plants in Japanese culture?

In Japanese culture, flowers and plants are inseparable from day to day activities and reflect our awareness of the changing seasons. Most Japanese women study flower arranging and decorate the alcoves of guest rooms with the flowers that are in season. Most of the hand-

CROSS-CULTURAL QUILTING

Kumiko Sudo's work has been described as a masterful combination of the traditional American quilt construction methods of piecing, layering, and appliqué, with the traditional Japanese stitching technique of sashiko. Although the way she expresses herself through these techniques is of course unique, and contemporary quiltmaking is comparatively new in Japan, all these techniques have been used for centuries. And the arts and crafts of the East and West have been influencing each other for quite some time.

QUILTING, *for example, holds together the layers of the traditional futon, which the Japanese use as both mattress and bed cover. Futons of the past were beautifully decorative and made either of silk (for the rich) or indigo-dyed and patterned cotton. Centuries ago the Chinese were among many Eastern peoples who wore quilted armor as protection against arrows and swords and quilted clothing as protection against the cold. It is believed that Crusaders in the eleventh century brought the idea of quilted garments to Europe and that these eventually led to quilted bed covers.*

PATCHWORK in Japan seems to have practical, religious, and aesthetic origins that interweave with and reinforce one another. On the practical side, there was the economic necessity of preserving and recycling precious fabrics, which at times were even used as currency, to pay tribute to emperors, and to reward good service. This tradition prevailed well into the 1800s because the Japanese government enforced a policy of national seclusion. In an effort to curtail Western influence, Japan was sealed off from the rest of the world. Trade with other nations ceased, and as a result, fabrics were hoarded.

According to Shinto, the indigenous religion in Japan, all things, including cloth, have a spirit. Historically the Japanese have revered and loved cloth, considering it a treasure to be cherished. Prolonging the life of an old fabric, such as through salvaging scraps to use in patchwork, came to be a spiritual exercise. To this day, transforming scraps into something that is useful and artistic exemplifies the Japanese idea of beauty. Buddhism, too, which arrived in Japan in the sixth century, encouraged the craft of patchwork. Buddhist monks took a vow of poverty and wore patched robes. The geometric, orderly design of the patches in Buddhist robes symbolized the patterns of the rice paddies in Buddha's native India. Patchwork cloths are still considered to be fine offerings in Buddhist temples.

▲ MY MOTHER WAS A FLOWER ARRANGEMENT INSTRUCTOR, AND WE ALWAYS HAD DIFFERENT FLOWERS IN OUR HOME EACH WEEK. HERE MY TWO ELDER SISTERS STAND BESIDE ONE OF MY MOTHER'S ARRANGEMENTS.

painted picture scrolls on the walls depict flowers, plants, and birds; they are changed from time to time in agreement with the four seasons. So are kimonos: Women wear kimonos with spring flower designs only in the spring, and summer flowers only during the summer. The same holds true for the daily use of dishes and tea cups. In addition, during the first seven days of the new year, the entrance of every house is decorated with ornaments arranged with pine trees, bamboo, and peach flowers. Each month is named for a flower, for example, *Botan* (peony) for January, *Ume* (peach blossom) for February, *Suisen* (daffodil) for March, and so on. Many Japanese treasure the art of Bonsai, the dwarf trees, because it gives one the feeling of communion with the cosmos. Japanese families are proud of their family crests, which are widely used as emblems on furniture, formal kimonos, and personal belongings. Of the 4,500 most used designs, more than half are derived from flowers and plants. The most significant crest is the sixteen petal chrysanthemum, which belongs to the Japanese Emperor. In the Heian period (794–1192), noble ladies' names were mostly adopted from flowers, and the images of flowers were imprinted on all of their belongings. Sometimes they fastened real flowers to fans inscribed with poems to their lovers. Few Westerners realize that to be a fine Samurai, one must possess not only martial arts skills but also be well versed in composing poems, playing musical instruments, performing the ritual of the tea ceremony, and arranging flowers.

What is the significance of flowers and plants in your life?

Flowers signify both happiness and sadness, life and death. In Japan, we have many observances each year relating to flowers and plants; for me, the most enjoyable event is the festival called *Tanabata Matsuri* because the whole family can participate. As the day approaches, each household prepares the stalk of a fresh bamboo tree with plenty of green leaves, or buys one from a vendor, and decorates the tree with colored cutout papers, ornaments, and papers inscribed with children's wishes (see the photograph on page 14). Usually, my brother was the bamboo tree provider, and my father was the chief architect of the cutouts. My father hung a sign on the tree describing me as a dexterous girl and then took a commemorative picture of the tree.

Another example involves one of my pets, a wirehaired fox terrier named Chako-Chan who had passed away due to old age. I found her by the magnolia tree in our front yard as if she were sleeping in the shade. With my sister's help, I buried this precious friend by the tree and covered her with many flowers. It became our ritual to remember our other little animal friends who gave us such joy and happiness during our tender years. Whenever the magnolia tree is in full bloom with such a wonderful fragrance, I see images of those little friends, and I feel their happiness in heaven. To console my sorrow, my sister gave me a book called *The Secret Garden*, and I was intrigued by the story for quite some time. Indeed I was so young and happy.

APPLIQUÉ AND EMBROIDERY *were less common than quilting and patchwork because the Japanese were so adept at decorating cloth with stencil and resist-dyeing. Traditionally, the aboriginal race called the Ainu were the appliquérs of Japan. In the middle of the eighteenth century, this island people developed a kind of appliqué technique using cotton cloth. The Ainu turned the wonderfully intricate symmetrical designs used in their wood carvings into cloth patterns, which they appliquéd onto their elm-bark fiber clothing. Some of their designs resemble the Hawaiian style of appliqué. As was the case with patchwork, this practical and decorative art reflected religious beliefs. Appliqué was considered to be "spiritual armor," and the Ainu believed that the more intricate the design, the more protection it provided the wearer against evil spirits.*

SASHIKO *is a type of decorative stitching that is a hybrid of embroidery and quilting. Sashiko means "little stabs" and was originally a simple running stitch used to repair and strengthen fabrics. The stitching was used to hold together several layers of the loose and flimsy cloth available at the time. The arrival of sturdier cotton cloth freed women to be more inventive with their stitchery, and sashiko designs became more decorative. Today, sashiko is still used to impart quilts with wonderful textures.*

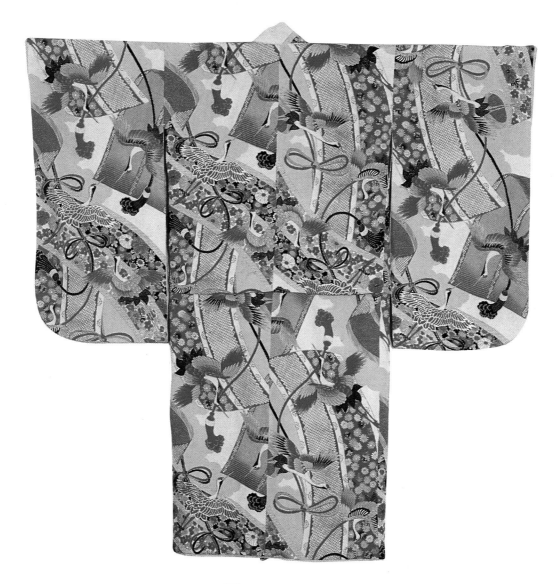

▲ THIS IS A GIRL'S KIMONO, AND THE DESIGN INCLUDES
CHRYSANTHEMUM FLOWERS, LONGEVITY CRANES, AND
COURT PALACE PARTITIONS.

▼ I HAD BEEN PLAYING OUTSIDE WITH MY FRIENDS WHEN
MY FATHER CALLED ME IN TO TAKE THIS PHOTOGRAPH.
AS YOU CAN SEE, AS A FIVE-YEAR-OLD CHILD, I WASN'T
TOO HAPPY TO BE POSING FOR THIS PICTURE.

When I was nine years old, I went to live with my aunt and uncle in Kamakura. There I studied many books on alpine plants, which were owned by my uncle. There were many types of flowers in the yard, but both my aunt and uncle favored one particular rose whose petals were thick and velvety with a dark red color. It was so mysterious in the morning dew. One sunny day, my aunt and I were in the garden enjoying the roses; she confided to me that she would prefer to have a single red rose at her funeral, rather than a large wreath. Many years later, she passed on, and I sent red roses similar to the ones we both had cherished at the house on the hill.

Your fabric choices are so unique — what advice about fabric selection would you give other quilters?

I hope people will realize from studying the designs in this book that it is not always necessary to buy the usual quilting fabric with small print designs. If you buy some fabrics with bold or dynamic designs, you will be surprised as to how useful and exciting such printed designs can be. When you see a fabric you really like, it is a good idea to buy at least a yard or so, even though you may not have an immediate use for it. In this way you can build a collection of fabrics that give you the most pleasure and satisfaction. In addition, keeping fabric from clothes that family members have once worn is an old but important tradition for quilters. Incorporating such fabrics really adds to the heart and spirit of one's work, and people and places will always be remembered with fondness and gratitude.

How do you choose your colors?

I use colors to express the variations in light seen at dawn, during the daytime, at sunset, and during the evening to create a feeling of space, depth, and height. I also create another pattern within the pattern by maneuvering printed fabrics.

In choosing colors, I just follow my intuition or the mood of the day. Spontaneity is very important to my work. I may pick up subtle color, or make the color more intense, or introduce strong contrast or less contrast — these all depend on how I react to the individual pattern at the time. I have over two thousand different fabrics. To make the process of choosing fabrics go more smoothly, I have cut a two-inch square of each and put these in color categories, such as blue, red, yellow. I arrange them by group and create a fabric palette, like an oil painter does. By trial and error, I find just the right fabric for each shape in the design.

Today, we are surrounded by an abundance of everything, including fabrics. Even with my two thousand fabrics, I often encounter problems with finding the right fabric for the right spot. When Picasso was young and living in poverty, his palette was very limited. Nevertheless he produced many great paintings full of pathos during his Blue and Rose periods. Whenever I think of this, I cannot help but admonish myself for my endless search for fabrics.

How would you describe the difference in your approach in designing this series of blocks compared with those in the first East Quilts West?

Since in this book the subject of the motif is limited to flowers, the colors tend to be brighter and more feminine. I also used more curved lines in relation to straight lines. Moreover, I created more asymmetrical

YOSEGIRE is a style, a technique, and a phenomenon that resembles the crazy-quilt type of patchwork that was the rage in the United States during the late 1800s. There are Japanese examples of this type of construction dating back hundreds of years. Although developed as a means of preserving precious fabrics, in the last half of the nineteenth century, women used yosegire *purely as a fun way to decorate cloth and screens with a variety of colors, shapes, and textures. The random organization of patches eventually became so popular in Japan that it began to be dyed onto fabric, and today it is used to decorate porcelain and papers, too. Decorative Japanese screens displayed in the United States in 1876 are credited with starting the crazy-quilt patchwork fad in this country.*

Quilts were not the only means of East-West cross-cultural influence. With the opening of Japan, many Western painters showed Japanese influence in their work, including Claude Monet, Toulouse-Lautrec, Vincent van Gogh, and James McNeill Whistler. The story and music from Puccini's Madame Butterfly *and Gilbert and Sullivan's* Mikado *would not exist had the composers not been exposed to Japanese culture.*

arrangements within the blocks and used a more complex technique to break up the surface and reveal further movement.

I selected each block carefully to illustrate a particular aesthetic and concept. The patterns are designed in a stylized form to reflect the diverse range of expression that exists in the real world of flowers.

When I create a new block or pattern, the process is always encouraged by minimal hints and suggestions I find in many things — scenes from my window as I play the piano, images or sounds at the ballet or opera, characters on TV programs, books, museums, the delicate curve of Victorian furniture. In creating floral

▼ MY FATHER DECORATED A BAMBOO TREE WITH CUT PAPER IN CELEBRATION OF *TANABATA MATSURI* FESTIVAL. AS A CHILD, I ALSO WANTED TO CUT OUT DECORATIONS WITH HIS BIG SCISSORS, BUT MY HANDS WERE TOO SMALL AND I CRIED. BECAUSE OF THIS I AM UNHAPPY IN THE PICTURE. ALSO, MY SISTER DISLIKED THE OLD-FASHIONED FLASH THAT MY FATHER USED IN TAKING PHOTOS AND ALWAYS TURNED HER HEAD AWAY FROM THE CAMERA.

Experts attribute the modern interest in quiltmaking in both the United States and Japan to an exhibit of antique quilts that toured in the 1970s. The antique fabrics charmed those who saw them and, in the words of one expert, "stirred a memory of a way of life that had seemed destined to be lost forever." She was talking of her Japanese countrywomen, but she might have meant American women as well. Japanese quilt designs have evolved over hundreds of years of cross-cultural influence, and now the United States and Japan are the two largest quilt markets in the world.

patterns, I tried to expand my imagination as if I were living in the region surrounding the flower, many years ago. As I was studying the origins of flowers, I found that each region has a different attitude toward flowers in terms of religion, customs, and folklore. Some of them are quite fascinating. For instance, the rose is considered to be the queen of flowers and connected with romance and love. In some countries, the rose is related to love for the dead. In Switzerland, the rose garden meant cemetery. In other cultures, the rose symbolized sin. The stories go on indefinitely.

In this book, I explain my process of transplanting the original flowers into my fabric garden and also add some interesting stories about the flowers' origins and significance. After months of design challenges and study, I am ready to show you my flower garden with pleasure. I hope the seeds of my thirty flower designs will fall on fertile soil and will bloom when their season comes.

▲ THIS KIMONO ONCE BELONGED TO MY AUNT BUT WAS REMADE INTO A CHILD'S *HAOREI* (OVERCOAT). THE DESIGN IS THAT OF PEONY FLOWERS AND *TEMARI* (CHILDREN'S SILK HANDBALLS).

▼ THIS PHOTOGRAPH SHOWS ME AND MY BEST FRIENDS IN FRONT OF OUR SCHOOL IN THE SPRING, ENJOYING THE CHERRY BLOSSOM SEASON.

HOW TO USE THIS BOOK

In this book you will find

SIX QUILT DESIGNS including
- a color photo and diagram of each quilt
- a color photo and diagram of each block
- step-by-step piecing instructions with drawings
- fabric requirements for a variety of quilt sizes
- template patterns for each block
- metric equivalents for all measurements

TWENTY-FOUR ADDITIONAL BLOCK DESIGNS including
- a color photo and diagram of each block
- step-by-step piecing instructions
- template patterns for each block
- metric equivalents for all measurements

In other words, a total of thirty new designs will inspire, excite, and delight you.

WHERE TO BEGIN

As you look through its pages, you'll notice that *East Quilt West II* is not like other quilting books. The designs and the fabrics are a meeting of Eastern and Western design, color, and culture. We invite you to explore this Eastern culture as fully as you like. As you are reading, perhaps you might burn some incense and sip a cup of green tea. Or find an album of Japanese music to provide more Japanese atmosphere. If you've never had sushi, this may be the perfect time to try it. Experiment with origami (the Japanese art of paper folding). A bit of experience will make it easier for you to follow the origami-like step-by-step drawings that accompany the instructions for the quilts.

Learning more about *ikebana*, the art of Japanese flower arrangement, will help you understand and appreciate Kumiko's sense of design. To a Westerner's eye, Japanese flower arrangements may seem at first to be unbalanced because the design principles used are different. A successful arrangement, however, possesses an underlying meaning and aesthetically pleasing order based on Confucian concepts. While these suggestions are not essential, they will help you better understand and enter into the spirit of Kumiko's quilts.

Some of the designs may look puzzling at first, almost off-balance, as if the blocks were cut up and tossed around. In addition, to create the completed quilts, Kumiko has flipped, mirrored, and rotated some of the units that create the blocks. The fabric color and pattern combinations are often like nothing we've ever seen before. But as you study them, their unique beauty, harmony, subtlety, and logic becomes clearer.

In the past, Kumiko used silk from old Japanese garments to make quilts. In this book, all the fabrics in the blocks and quilts are contemporary American fabrics. Yet in many cases, the overall effect still reflects a Japanese sensibility. Since the fabrics are available in the United States, you can probably duplicate the fabric choices. However, Kumiko feels that color is an individual expression, and her choices are for inspiration, not instruction. In Japan, certain colors and design patterns have symbolic meaning, and these are part of Kumiko's cultural heritage. In addition, the Japanese approach to color and design is often extemporaneous and straightforward, while emphasizing contrast or conflict that creates a startling density and depth. This cultural history of color makes her approach different from traditional quilting and is, she feels, what gives her quilts their unique character. So, you can make a "Kumiko quilt" or make one that has your own imprint on it.

POINTERS ON TECHNIQUE

This book is different not only in design and spirit but also in technical matters. To ensure successful and pleasurable quiltmaking, keep the following in mind:

■ This book is for people who have at least basic skills in quiltmaking. If you are new to this craft, you should first familiarize yourself through a book such as *Quilts! Quilts!! Quilts!!!*

■ Advanced quilters should have no problems with any of the thirty designs. Six of the blocks also include instructions for making complete quilts in various sizes. These include detailed how-to illustrations that accompany the step-by-step instructions for making the block. Beginners are best advised to start with one of these illustrated blocks to familiarize themselves with Kumiko's methods of sewing. Then you can go on to make other blocks more easily, comfortably, and confidently. Beginning and intermediate quilters will also find it easier to first try blocks with fewer curved seams.

■ Full-size templates for all blocks are provided at the back of the book. All templates and measurements include a ¼" (6mm) seam allowance, unless otherwise indicated. Several of the templates need to be reversed for cutting fabric pieces, as indicated on the templates. Take special care in these cases. Mark the reversed pieces to avoid confusion.

■ In some blocks, smaller pieces are appliquéd onto background fabric. Placement will be more accurate if you make a separate set of templates without seam allowance. Referring to the diagram for your quilt block, position the placement templates on the background fabric and draw around them. Use these pencil lines to guide your appliqué.

■ Many quilters are skilled at sewing curved seams by machine, but others prefer to tackle them by hand sewing. Kumiko prefers to use a form of appliqué for curved seams. This technique involves placing a fabric piece, with the seam allowance folded under, on top of a second piece; the fold is placed along the seamline of the lower piece and blind stitched by hand. The word *appliqué* in the instructions means to use this method when curved seams are involved. The term *sew* indicates the traditional method of sewing pieces together, right sides facing, using a running stitch on the wrong side along the seamline. Straight seams are sewn together this way, and you may use hand or machine stitching. Kumiko stitches everything — curved and straight seams — by hand. Although it's "okay" for others to sew by machine, she feels that the hand is directed not only by the eye but also by the heart. Furthermore, for Kumiko, the machine puts a distance between her and the work.

■ The fabric charts specify the precise amount of material needed to complete the quilt blocks. But it's always a good idea to buy more in case of mishap. It is far better to have a bit too much fabric than a bit too little.

■ The fabric amounts for borders on the quilts are figured without piecing if they are over 2" (5cm) wide. To save fabric, narrower borders are figured as pieced. Of course, the decision to piece or not to piece is up to you. Sometimes the border is one of the fabrics that appears in the block; in this case, you may want to use the waste fabric from the border to make the block pieces. Notice that Kumiko uses two assembly techniques to attach the borders — overlapped and edge to edge.

■ Instructions are given for making block and quilt tops only. To finish your project, you will need to buy batting and backing fabric, assemble the layers, and quilt them together. Kumiko considers quilting to be an accent "rather than something to be seen all over the picture." She usually uses silk thread to decorate her quilt tops with *sashiko*-style Japanese embroidery. In quilts used as wall hangings, such accent stitching will suffice; however, quilts used as bedding will require more extensive quilting. Kumiko seldom draws a design but usually quilts "freestyle." In some of the designs in this book, she followed the line of the pattern block, stitching ⅛" (3mm) away from the seamline. She rarely uses thread to match the fabric — for example, she often uses purple thread for yellow fabric and green for blue fabric — and may use two or three different thread colors in one quilt.

■ Experiment. Use your imagination. You may want to make a whole quilt or make several individual blocks in different designs. The generous 16" × 16" (41cm × 41cm) finished block size makes them ideal for small wall hangings, pillows, or other projects. You can also add to or subtract from the width and number of borders in a quilt top to get a variety of effects and sizes.

BLOCKS

AND

QUILTS

CAMELLIA

In front of my aunt's house grew several camellia trees. I clearly remember standing near these trees, with the rain falling on the flowers, and seeing thousands of petals covering the ground like a gorgeous carpet.

The camellia was named after a Jesuit priest, G. J. Kamel, who traveled to Asia in the seventeenth century. The camellia originated in Japan, China, and Korea and was brought to the United States in the eighteenth century by explorers. The hundreds of varieties we see today are mostly hybrids of Camellia Japonica. It is now the state flower of Alabama. In this block, I depicted camellias in full bloom by a window on a cold winter day with snow outside.

INSTRUCTIONS
Templates on page 78.

To make the block, cut the required number of pieces indicated on the templates. To assemble the block, sew the pieces together in the following sequence, using the diagram as a guide.

1. Sew C and B together.
2. Sew A onto No. 1.
3. Appliqué D and F onto No. 2.
4. Appliqué E and G onto No. 3.
5. Appliqué H onto No. 4.
6. Appliqué I onto No. 5.
7. Appliqué J onto No. 6.
8. Appliqué K onto No. 7.
9. Appliqué two L's onto No. 8.
10. Appliqué M onto No. 9
11. Repeat the above steps to make four squares. Sew the squares together.

Finished block size: 16" × 16" (41cm × 41cm)

PRIMROSE

The primrose symbolizes youth, and sometimes as I walked home from school I would pick a small bouquet of primroses to give to my mother.

The primrose has many sweetly scented flowers grouped on one stem, which resembles a bundle of keys. Thus it is called the "flower of the goddess," because she opens the doors of the spring season with the keys she carries. I used a light blue dotted print to represent the early spring sky as a backdrop for an abundance of colorful primroses.

INSTRUCTIONS
Templates on page 80.

To make the block, cut the required number of pieces indicated on the templates. To assemble the block, sew the pieces together in the following sequence, using the diagram as a guide.

1. Piece A is an 8½" (22cm) square. This includes seam allowance.
2. Lay out all placement templates on piece A and draw guidelines.
3. Appliqué B, C, and D to A.
4. Appliqué two E's, two F's, and two G's onto No. 3.
5. Appliqué H between the two G's.
6. Appliqué two I's, two J's, and two K's onto No. 5.
7. Appliqué two L's onto No. 6.
8. Appliqué two M's onto No. 7.
9. Appliqué two N's onto No. 8.
10. Appliqué O between the two N's.
11. Repeat the above steps to make four squares. Sew the squares together.

Finished block size: 16" × 16" (41cm × 41cm)

MAGNOLIA

When I was about five years old, my friends and I would collect magnolia petals and use them as make-believe plates. Or we would tie them together to make garlands to wear around our necks.

The magnolia is one of the most beautiful flowering trees in the southern United States. In China it is the flower of May and the symbol of feminine sweetness. To recreate the magnificence of the flower, I used a brilliant red floral print as the main motif. A combination of green, blue-green, and purple at the four corners represents its sturdy and shiny foliage.

INSTRUCTIONS
Templates on page 81.

To make the block, cut the required number of pieces indicated on the templates. To assemble the block, sew the pieces together in the following sequence, using the diagram as a guide.

1. Piece A is a 16½" (42cm) square. This includes seam allowance.
2. Lay out all placement templates on one corner of piece A and draw guidelines.
3. Appliqué two D's onto A and then two C's.
4. Appliqué B between the two C's.
5. Appliqué two E's onto No. 4.
6. Appliqué two F's onto No. 5.
7. Appliqué two G's onto No. 6.
8. Appliqué H onto No. 7.
9. Repeat the above steps in each of the remaining corners of the background square.

Finished block size: 16" × 16" (41cm × 41cm)

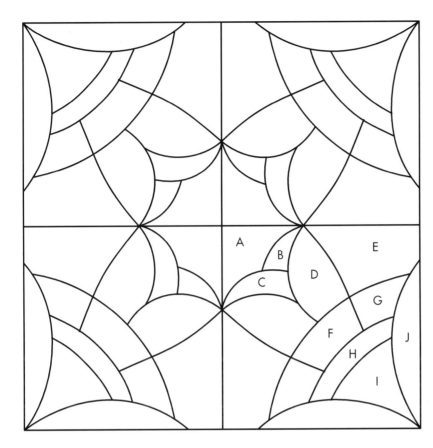

FUCHSIA

Many years ago, I thought fuchsias resembled beautifully dressed ballerinas dancing in the sky. With all those beautiful dancing creatures, I imagined I was in some sort of natural fantasy land.

This tropical shrub most likely originated in Mexico, Chile, or Argentina. The many varieties of fuchsias seen in home gardens today are mostly hybrids of the original species. I created my own hybrid by stylizing the flower.

INSTRUCTIONS
Templates on page 83.

To make one block, cut the required number of pieces indicated on the templates. Cutting instructions for making a quilt, and assembly instructions for making a block or a quilt are given on the following pages.

Finished block size: 16" × 16" (41cm × 41cm)

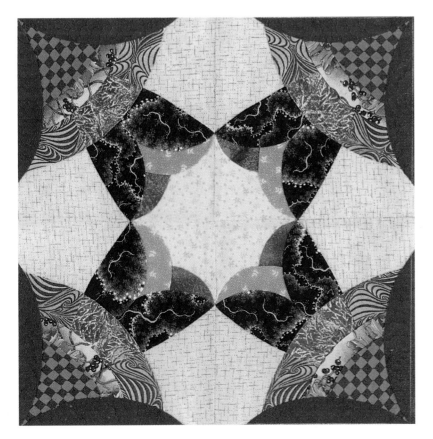

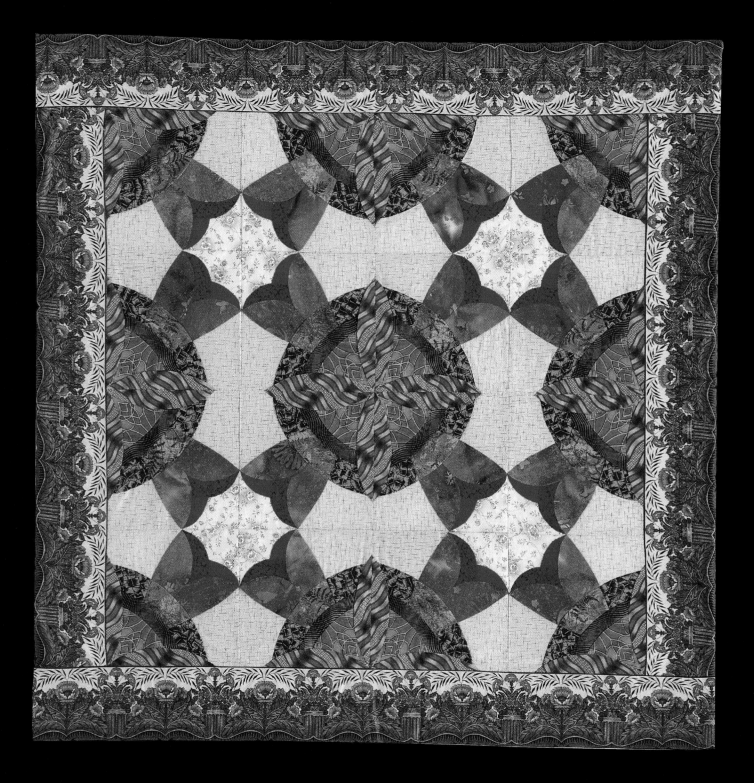

FUCHSIA: *Quilt*

	WALL/CRIB	TWIN	DOUBLE/QUEEN	KING
Size (inches)	40 × 40	72 × 88	88 × 88	104 × 104
Size (centimeters)	102 × 102	183 × 224	224 × 224	264 × 264
Setting	2 × 2	4 × 5	5 × 5	6 × 6
Blocks	4	20	25	36

Fabric needed: *Yards (centimeters) for 45" (114cm) fabric*

	WALL/CRIB	TWIN	DOUBLE/QUEEN	KING
Template A	¼ (23)	⅞ (80)	1⅛ (103)	1½ (137)
Template B	⅛ (11)	⅝ (57)	¾ (69)	1 (91)
Template C	¼ (23)	¾ (69)	⅞ (80)	1¼ (114)
Template D	⅜ (34)	1⅞ (171)	2⅜ (213)	3⅜ (309)
Template E	⅝ (57)	2⅞ (263)	3½ (320)	5 (457)
Template F	¼ (23)	¾ (69)	⅞ (80)	1¼ (114)
Template G	¼ (23)	1⅛ (103)	1½ (137)	2 (183)
Template H	¼ (23)	¾ (69)	1 (91)	1⅜ (304)
Template I	¼ (23)	1 (91)	1¼ (114)	1¾ (160)
Template J	½ (46)	2¼ (206)	2⅞ (263)	4 (366)
Border	¾ (69)	2⅝ (240)	2⅝ (240)	3 (274)

Cutting

	WALL/CRIB	TWIN	DOUBLE/QUEEN	KING
Template A	16	80	100	144
Template B	16	80	100	144
Template C	16	80	100	144
Template D	32	160	200	288
Template E	32	160	200	288
Template F	16	80	100	144
Template G	32	160	200	288
Template H	16	80	100	144
Template I	16	80	100	144
Template J	32	160	200	288

Border width is 4½" (11cm) including ¼" (6mm) seam allowance.

1.

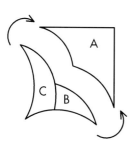

2.

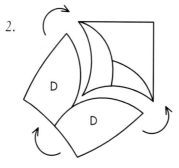

ASSEMBLY INSTRUCTIONS

To assemble each block, sew the pieces together in the following sequence, using the step-by-step drawings and the diagram as guides.

1. Appliqué B onto C and then appliqué onto A.
2. Sew two D's together. Open the seam and appliqué onto No. 1.
3. Sew two E's to No. 2.
4. Sew two G's to F and then appliqué onto No. 3.
5. Appliqué H onto No. 4.
6. Appliqué I onto No. 5.
7. Appliqué two J's onto No. 6.
8. Repeat the above steps to make four squares. Sew the squares together.

To make this quilt, assemble and sew together the number of blocks required to complete your project. For example, the quilt shown here is wall hanging size with four blocks sewn together in two rows of two plus one border.

3.

4.

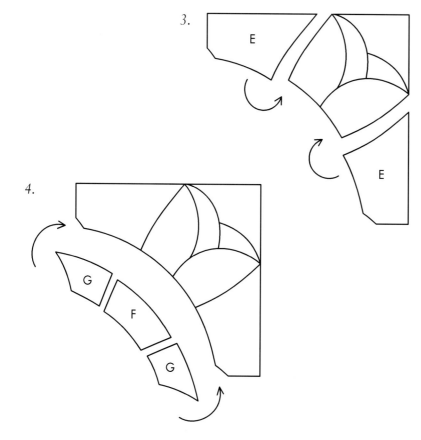

5. and 6.

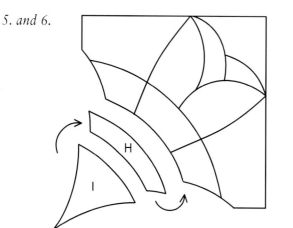

7.

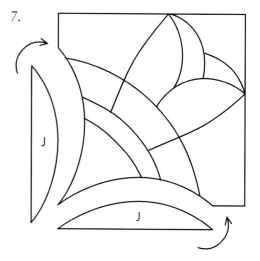

THISTLE

Some people don't like the thistle, but I like it very much because its shape is so unique and it has such a beautiful color. When I was a child, my friends and I would collect dry thistle flowers, take them to the top of a hill, and have fun releasing the parachute seeds into the wind. Today, my garden always seems to have a few thistle plants that I never planted. The flowers of the thistle plant range from pink to purple, yellow, and white. They are rich in nectar for bees and butterflies.

During the reign of Malcolm I, the thistle was adopted as the Scottish emblem. When an army of Norsemen attempted to attack Scottish forces by night, one of the soldiers stepped on a thistle and cried out. The aroused Scots defeated the invaders.

In this design, I placed a thistle at each of the four corners and the sharp leaves and spines in the center of the block.

INSTRUCTIONS
Templates on page 85.

To make the block, cut the required number of pieces indicated on the templates. To assemble the block, sew the pieces together in the following sequence, using the diagram as a guide.

1. Appliqué F onto G.
2. Sew a C to either side of D.
3. Sew a B to each C.
4. Sew an A to each B.
5. Appliqué No. 4 onto G.
6. Appliqué E onto No. 5.
7. Repeat the above steps to make four squares. Sew the squares together.

Finished block size: 16" × 16" (41cm × 41cm)

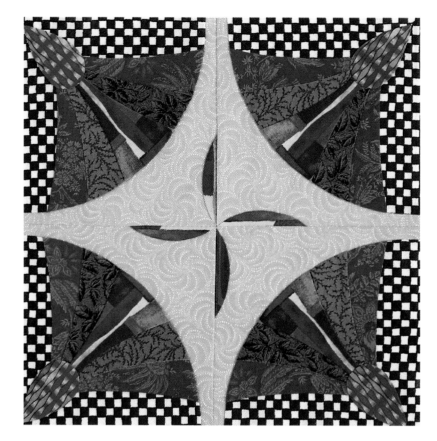

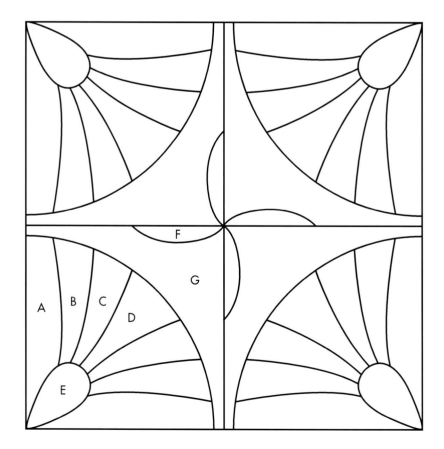

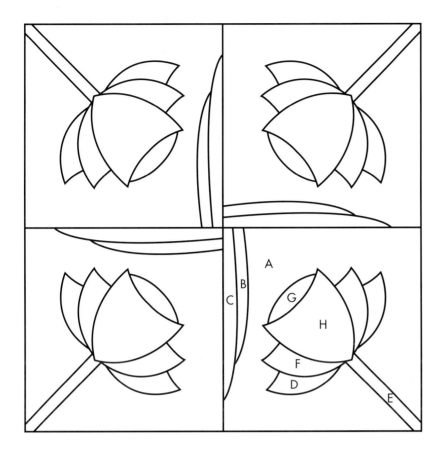

CROWN IMPERIAL

One autumn day, my mother and I went to her hometown to visit the grave of my grandfather. On our way, we stopped and picked some crown imperial flowers growing near a rice field. We put the flowers on his grave, making this a day that I will probably never forget.

The crown imperial is said to have originated in western Asia. This vigorous and decorative flower has numerous sessile leaves, but for this design, I placed the leaves in the center of the block, separated from the stem. In accordance with its noble name, I used orange and reddish colors, which were believed to be used only by high priests and noblemen in ancient Japan.

INSTRUCTIONS
Templates on page 87.

To make the block, cut the required number of pieces indicated on the templates. To assemble the block, sew the pieces together in the following sequence, using the diagram as a guide.

1. Piece A is an 8½" (22cm) square. This includes seam allowance.
2. Lay out all placement templates on A and draw guidelines.
3. Appliqué B and C onto A.
4. Appliqué E and G onto No. 3.
5. Appliqué two D's onto No. 4.
6. Appliqué two F's onto No. 5.
7. Appliqué H between the two F's and over G.
8. Repeat the above steps to make four squares. Sew the squares together.

Finished block size: 16" × 16" (41cm × 41cm)

COCKSCOMB

During my tenth summer, my mother and I took a two-day train ride to the northern part of Japan to visit my grandmother. There was a henhouse nearby, and I can still picture in my mind the evening scene of chickens pecking among the shadows of the trees and the cockscomb flowers.

The cockscomb is an eye-catching summer flower because of its brilliant color and its shape resembling a crest. To create a great many tiny bright flowers, I used three different shades of red; plenty of greens and blues provide complimentary colors.

INSTRUCTIONS
Templates on page 88.

To make the block, cut the required number of pieces indicated on the templates. To assemble the block, sew the pieces together in the following sequence, using the diagram as a guide.

1. Appliqué B, C, and D onto A.
2. Appliqué two H's onto No. 1.
3. Appliqué E, F, and G onto No. 2.
4. Appliqué two I's onto No. 3.
5. Sew two J's together along the straight edge. Open the seam and then appliqué onto No. 4.
6. Repeat the above steps to make four squares. Sew the squares together.

Finished block size: 16" × 16" (41cm × 41cm)

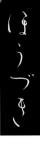

CHINESE LANTERN

Also called winter cherry, this unusual-looking plant develops a paper-thin orange-red fruit on each pedicel in early summer. In downtown Tokyo, row after row of the plants are auctioned to thousands of admirers, providing a sure sign that the summer season has begun. I recall sitting on the backseat of my father's bicycle one hot August, riding to the chinese lantern market. There were beautiful baskets filled with the flowers, and we found the most lovely flower arrangement to take home with us. What a wonderful day!

This block design suggests chinese lanterns dangling from strings and swaying in the wind on a summer evening.

INSTRUCTIONS
Templates on page 90.

To make the block, cut the required number of pieces indicated on the templates. To assemble the block, sew the pieces together in the following sequence, using the diagram as a guide.

1. Appliqué B, C, D, E, and F onto A.
2. Sew two G's together along the straight edge. Open the seam and appliqué onto No. 1.
3. Appliqué two H's onto No. 2.
4. Appliqué two I's onto No. 3.
5. Sew two J's together along the straight edge. Open the seam and appliqué onto No. 4.
6. Repeat the above steps to make four squares. Sew the squares together.

Finished block size: 16" × 16" (41cm × 41cm)

HONEYSUCKLE

Honeysuckle is a climbing shrub with very fragrant flowers that look to me like flying birds. Once, when my sister and I went to look for seashells near our home, we walked past many honeysuckle plants that had shed their petals. We started to pick up the petals, and soon we had a paper bag full of them — and we completely forgot about collecting seashells.

Here, I interpreted the honeysuckle by exaggerating its tubulous flowers to express its movement. Two shades of yellowish backgrounds accentuate the brilliance of the flowers.

INSTRUCTIONS
Templates on page 92.

To make the block, cut the required number of pieces indicated on the templates. To assemble the block, sew the pieces together in the following sequence, using the diagram as a guide.

1. Piece A is an 8½" (22cm) square. This includes seam allowance.
2. Lay out all placement templates on piece A and draw guidelines. Then appliqué B and C onto A.
3. Appliqué two D's onto No. 2.
4. Appliqué two E's onto No. 3.
5. Sew F onto No. 4, using a basting stitch, without folding in seam allowances.
6. Appliqué G onto No. 5.
7. Appliqué H onto No. 6.
8. Repeat the above steps to make four squares. Sew the squares together.

Finished block size: 16" × 16" (41cm × 41cm)

EGYPTIAN LOTUS

I longed to see Egyptian lotus flowers, but when I visited Egypt there were none to be seen. Instead, I saw many lotus designs carved in ancient stone buildings, and these made me feel as though I had gone back three thousand years. Later, I put my hand in the Nile and the circular ripples reminded me of the lotus flower.

In Egypt, the lotus represents the resurrection of the god Osiris and his sister-wife Isis. Egyptian mummies often held a lotus in their hands as a symbol of new life. In China, it is the emblem of longevity. In this block, I used a blue floral print to evoke the blue Nile. Reddish colored flowers suggest lotus flowers floating on the blue water.

INSTRUCTIONS
Templates on page 93.

To make one block, cut the required number of pieces indicated on the templates. Cutting instructions for making a quilt, and assembly instructions for making a block or a quilt are given on the following pages.

Finished block size: 16" × 16" (41cm × 41cm)

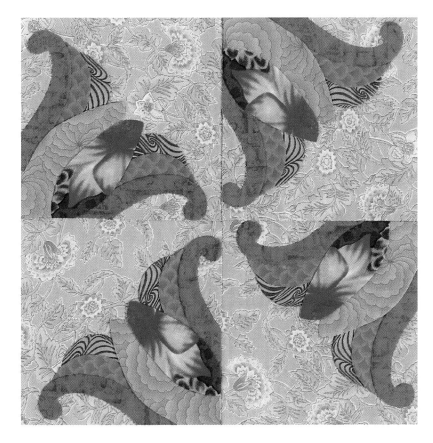

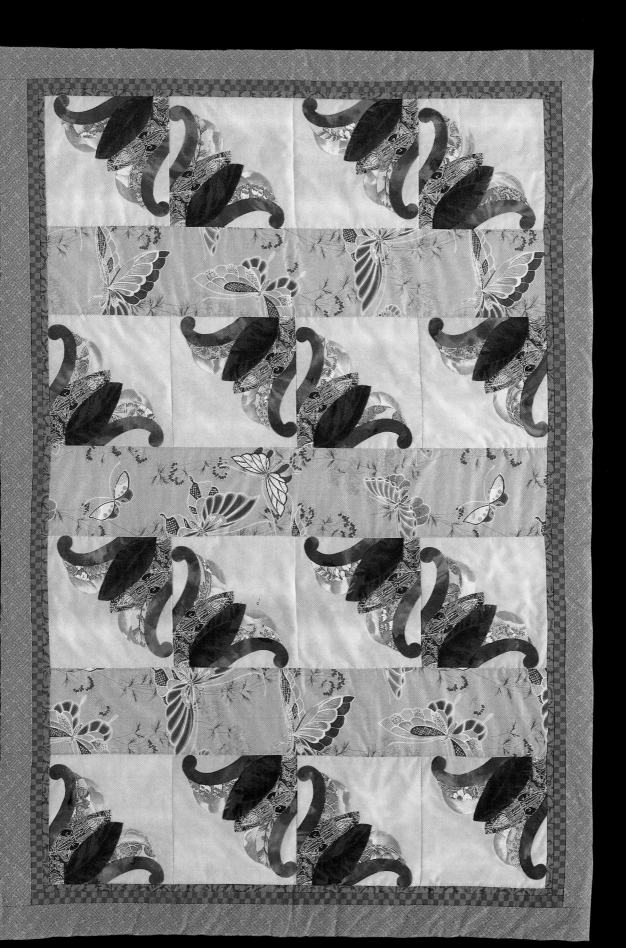

EGYPTIAN LOTUS: *Quilt*

	WALL/CRIB	TWIN	DOUBLE/QUEEN	KING
Size (inches)	37 × 57	71 × 85	87 × 85	119 × 114
Size (centimeters)	94 × 145	180 × 216	221 × 216	302 × 290
Setting	4 × 4	8 × 6	10 × 6	14 × 8
Quarter blocks	16	48	60	112
Horizontal bars	3	5	5	7

Fabric needed: *Yards (centimeters) for 45" (114cm) fabric*

	WALL/CRIB	TWIN	DOUBLE/QUEEN	KING
Template A	¾ (69)	2¼ (206)	2¾ (251)	5 (457)
Template B	¼ (23)	¾ (69)	⅞ (80)	1⅝ (149)
Template C	¼ (23)	¾ (69)	1 (91)	1¾ (160)
Template D	⅝ (57)	1⅝ (149)	2 (183)	3½ (320)
Template E	¼ (23)	¾ (69)	1 (91)	1¾ (160)
Template F	¼ (23)	¾ (69)	⅞ (80)	1⅝ (149)
Horizontal bars	⅝ (57)	2 (183)	2¼ (206)	3½ (320)
First border	½ (46)	¾ (69)	¾ (69)	1 (91)
Second border	½ (46)	1 (91)	1 (91)	1 (91)
Third border	1⅝ (149)	2½ (229)	2½ (229)	3½ (320)

Cutting

	WALL/CRIB	TWIN	DOUBLE/QUEEN	KING
Template A	16	48	60	112
Template B	32	96	120	224
Template C	32	96	120	224
Template D	32	96	120	224
Template E	16	48	60	112
Template F	16	48	60	112

Horizontal bar width is 6½" (17cm) including ¼" (6mm) seam allowance.

First border width is 1½" (4cm) including ¼" (6mm) seam allowance.
Second border width is 2" (5cm) including ¼" (6mm) seam allowance.
Third border width is 3" (8cm) including ¼" (6mm) seam allowance.

3.

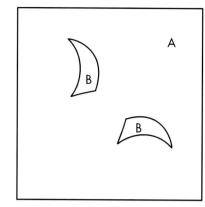

4.

5.

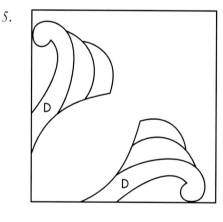

6.

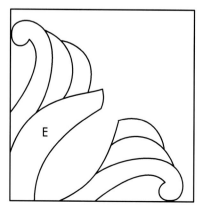

7.

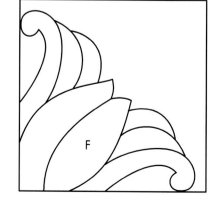

ASSEMBLY INSTRUCTIONS

To assemble each block, sew the pieces together in the following sequence, using the step-by-step drawings and the diagram as guides.

1. Piece A is an 8½" (22cm) square. This includes seam allowance.
2. Lay out all placement templates on A and draw guidelines.
3. Appliqué two B's onto A.
4. Appliqué two C's onto No. 3.
5. Appliqué two D's onto No. 4.
6. Appliqué E onto No. 5.
7. Appliqué F onto No. 6.
8. Repeat the above steps to make four squares (quarter blocks). Sew the squares together.

In this quilt, the squares (quarter blocks) are sewn together in strips instead of blocks and are set with solid bars of fabric. Note that the orientation of adjacent quarter blocks differs from that in the full block. Assemble and sew together the number of quarter blocks required to complete your project. For example, the quilt shown here is wall hanging size with sixteen quarter blocks sewn in four rows of four quarter blocks each with three horizontal bars and two borders.

CORNFLOWER

I have always loved the cornflower because it was part of a daily family ritual. My mother would put the flowers on a religious altar we had in our home, and I would put a small offering on the altar while smelling the incense and looking at the flowers.

The cornflower is native to southern Europe, where we find masses of blue, purple, pink, or white flowers amidst the cornfields in spring and summer. In this block, I simplified the florets as a linear design. The greenish background represents a vast wild field, and the center triangles signify individual florets in the wind.

INSTRUCTIONS
Templates on page 94.

To make the block, cut the required number of pieces indicated on the templates. To assemble the block, sew the pieces together in the following sequence, using the diagram as a guide.

1. Appliqué two B's onto G.
2. Sew two A's and a B together.
3. Sew an F to either side of No. 2 and sew to G.
4. Sew an E to either side of C and sew to No. 3.
5. Sew D to No. 4.
6. Repeat the above steps to make four squares. Sew the squares together.

Finished block size: 16" × 16" (41cm × 41cm)

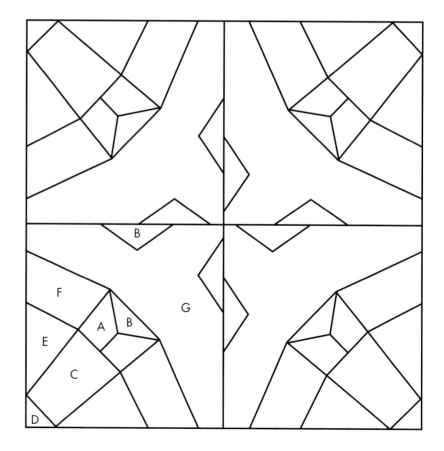

FLAME TREE

One summer vacation, I was in Bangkok sitting on a bench under a flame tree with its beautiful red blossoms. I remember hearing the laughter of girls I could see in their traditional dresses, riding bicycles. The wind was very soft and gentle to my cheeks.

This design recalls that day with its brilliant red flowers facing outward and its strongly contrasting dark green leaves in the center. This passionately colored tree grows in abundance in South America and Southeast Asia, where it originated.

INSTRUCTIONS
Templates on page 95.

To make the block, cut the required number of pieces indicated on the templates. To assemble the block, sew the pieces together in the following sequence, using the diagram as a guide.

1. Piece A is an 8½" (22cm) square. This includes seam allowance.
2. Lay out all placement templates on A and draw guidelines.
3. Sew B and C together and appliqué onto A.
4. Appliqué two D's onto No. 3.
5. Appliqué E between the two D's.
6. Appliqué two F's onto No. 5.
7. Appliqué two G's onto No. 6.
8. Appliqué two H's onto No. 7.
9. Appliqué I between the two H's.
10. Repeat the above steps to make four squares. Sew the squares together.

Finished block size: 16" × 16" (41cm × 41cm)

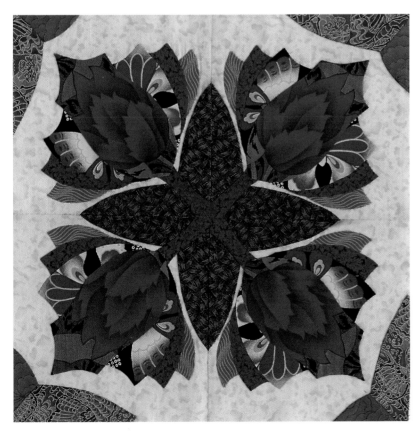

DAFFODIL

My aunt had an enormous decorative stone in her garden and around it many yellow daffodils bloomed each spring. Sometimes I sat on the stone like an old man, just enjoying the beauty of the flowers all around me.

The daffodil is a type of narcissus, a flower that gets its name from the Greek myth in which the youth Narcissus fell in love with his own image reflected in a pond. Upon his death — due to unfulfilled love — he was transformed into a flower. The narcissus is well known for its beautiful appearance and fragrance. In this block, I tried to capture the image of Narcissus leaning toward the water to admire his reflection.

INSTRUCTIONS
Templates on page 97.

To make the block, cut the required number of pieces indicated on the templates. To assemble the block, sew the pieces together in the following sequence, using the diagram as a guide.

1. Appliqué two B's onto A.
2. Appliqué D and E onto No. 1.
3. Appliqué two C's onto No. 2.
4. Sew two F's together along the straight edge, then open the seam and appliqué onto No. 3.
5. Appliqué two G's onto No. 4.
6. Appliqué two H's onto No. 5.
7. Appliqué I onto No. 6.
8. Repeat the above steps to make four squares. Sew the squares together.

Finished block size: 16" × 16" (41cm × 41cm)

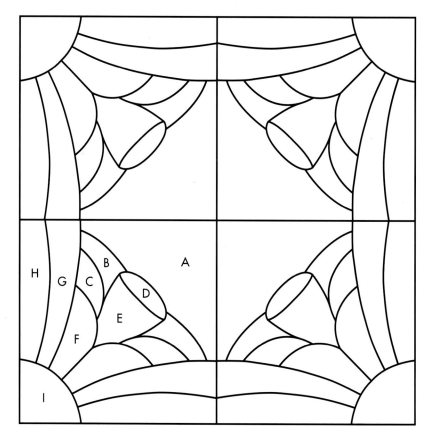

CALLA LILY

During one summer vacation, my brother and I went fishing in a nearby river. I walked toward a group of cattails and found a few short calla lilies; on one of them sat a tiny green frog. As I reached to pick up the frog, it jumped away and I fell into the mud. My mother was not too happy when we got home!

The calla lily originated in South Africa, and its large shapely tubes make it one of the most popular flowers today. Instead of using white, I took the liberty of manipulating many vibrant colors to enhance the design. The pink background represents the anticipation of springtime, and the orange represents the fulfillment of summer, the calla lily's blooming period.

INSTRUCTIONS
Templates on page 99.

To make one block, cut the required number of pieces indicated on the templates. Cutting instructions for making a quilt, and assembly instructions for making a block or a quilt are given on the following pages.

Finished block size: 16" × 16" (41cm × 41cm)

CALLA LILY: *Quilt*

	WALL/CRIB	TWIN	DOUBLE/QUEEN	KING
Size (inches)	38 × 38	70 × 86	86 × 86	102 × 102
Size (centimeters)	97 × 97	178 × 218	218 × 218	259 × 259
Setting	2 × 2	4 × 5	5 × 5	6 × 6
Blocks	4	20	25	36

Fabric needed: *Yards (centimeters) for 45" (114cm) fabric*

Template A	¾ (69)	3⅜ (309)	4½ (411)	6½ (594)
Template B	¼ (23)	⅞ (80)	1⅛ (103)	1½ (137)
Template C	⅛ (11)	⅝ (57)	¾ (69)	1⅛ (103)
Template D	¼ (23)	¾ (69)	⅞ (80)	1¼ (114)
Template E	½ (46)	2 (183)	2½ (229)	3½ (320)
Template F	⅜ (34)	1⅞ (171)	2¼ (206)	3¼ (297)
First border	1⅛ (103)	2½ (229)	2½ (229)	3 (274)
Second border	¼ (23)	¾ (69)	¾ (69)	1 (91)

Cutting

Template A	16	80	100	144
Template B	16	80	100	144
Template C	16	80	100	144
Template D	16	80	100	144
Template E	16	80	100	144
Template F	16	80	100	144

First border width is 2½" (6cm) including ¼" (6mm) seam allowance.
Second border width is 1½" (4cm) including ¼" (6mm) seam allowance.

3.

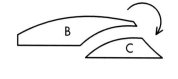

4.

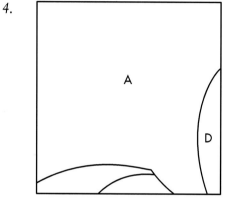

5.

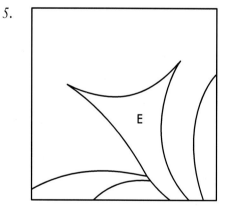

6.

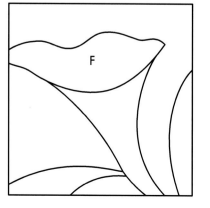

To assemble each block, sew the pieces together in the following sequence, using the step-by-step drawings and the diagram as guides.

1. Piece A is an 8½" (22cm) square. This includes seam allowance.
2. Layout all placement templates on A and draw guidelines.
3. Appliqué B onto C.
4. Appliqué No. 3 and D onto A.
5. Appliqué E onto No. 4.
6. Appliqué F onto No. 5.
7. Repeat the above steps to make four squares. Sew the squares together.

To make this quilt, assemble and sew together the number of blocks required to complete your project. For example, the quilt shown here is wall hanging size with four blocks sewn together in two rows of two plus two borders. Note that this size lends itself to an unusual assembly pattern. In each block one square has been turned to create the effect of a full block floating in the center.

LILY OF THE VALLEY

My mother's favorite flower is the lily of the valley because so many of them grow in the part of Japan where she was born. After living many years in Tokyo, she sometimes bought a small pot of these flowers to put on her windowsill. A few years ago she sent me some lily of the valley made out of paper (origami), and they will bloom in my studio forever.

The lily of the valley is associated with the Virgin Mary in the Christian religion. The exquisite small, white, bell-shaped flowers hang in a one-sided cluster and sweeten the air with perfume in late spring. In this design, different values of blue form the background and enhance the lighter-colored flower blooming quietly in the spring air.

INSTRUCTIONS
Templates on page 100.

To make the block, cut the required number of pieces indicated on the templates. To assemble the block, sew the pieces together in the following sequence, using the diagram as a guide.

1. Piece A is an 8½" (22cm) square. This includes seam allowance.
2. Lay out all placement templates on A and draw guidelines.
3. Appliqué B, C, and D onto A.
4. Appliqué three F's onto No. 3.
5. Appliqué two E's onto each F.
6. Repeat the above steps to make four squares. Sew the squares together.

Finished block size: 16" × 16" (41cm × 41cm)

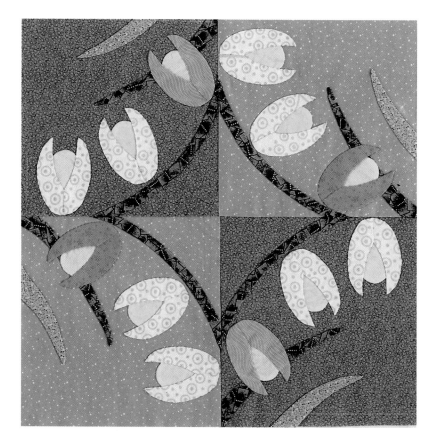

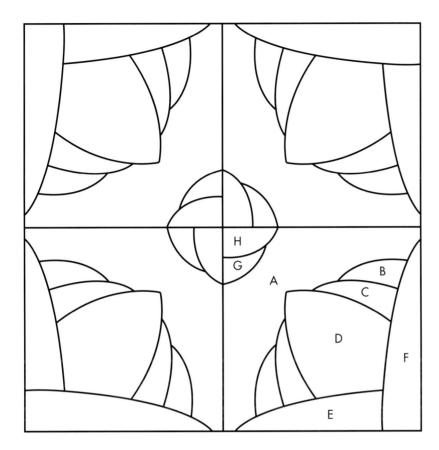

PEONY

The peony is one of the most popular flowers in China as well as Japan, and the motif is used frequently for silk screens, ceramics, paintings, and textiles. After New Year's Day some Japanese temples have a special open house to show their peony gardens. To protect them from the cold and snow, small straw shelters are built for each plant. What a beautiful sight to see the shelters covered with snow, each containing precious red and pink peony blossoms.

In China, the flower is a symbol of love and affection and is very popular as the flower of March. In this block I have tried to capture the beauty of the peony about to bloom.

INSTRUCTIONS
Templates on page 101.

To make the block, cut the required number of pieces indicated on the templates. To assemble the block, sew the pieces together in the following sequence, using the diagram as a guide.

1. Piece A is an 8½" (22cm) square. This includes seam allowance.
2. Lay out all placement templates on A and draw guidelines.
3. Appliqué G and H onto A.
4. Appliqué two B's onto No. 3.
5. Appliqué two C's onto No. 4.
6. Appliqué D between the two C's.
7. Appliqué E onto No. 6.
8. Appliqué F onto No. 7.
9. Repeat the above steps to make four squares. Sew the squares together.

Finished block size: 16" × 16" (41cm × 41cm)

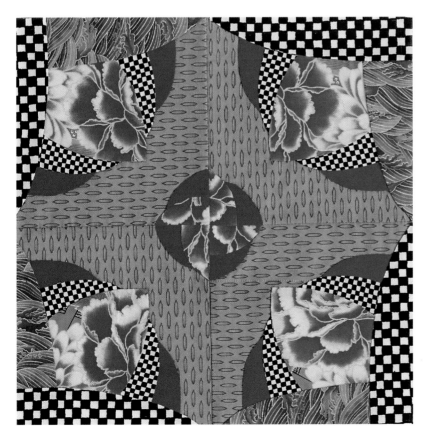

FRENCH LAVENDER

A native of the Mediterranean coast, French lavender is very popular because of its beautiful color and fragrance. This design depicts the flowers in deep shades of violet; they group together to form spikes, and emit a strong fragrance to entice the viewer's attention. I have also incorporated the silvery gray-green leaves. A white-gray background suggests the stony dry soil of the Mediterranean coast.

INSTRUCTIONS
Templates on page 102.

To make the block, cut the required number of pieces indicated on the templates. To assemble the block, sew the pieces together in the following sequence, using the diagram as a guide.

1. Piece A is an 8½" (22cm) square. This includes seam allowance.
2. Lay out all placement templates on A and draw guidelines.
3. Appliqué two B's onto A.
4. Appliqué two C's onto No. 3.
5. Appliqué two D's onto No. 4.
6. Appliqué two E's onto No. 5.
7. Appliqué F, G, and H onto No. 6.
8. Appliqué two I's onto No. 7.
9. Appliqué J onto No. 8.
10. Repeat the above steps to make four squares. Sew the squares together.

Finished block size: 16" × 16" (41cm × 41cm)

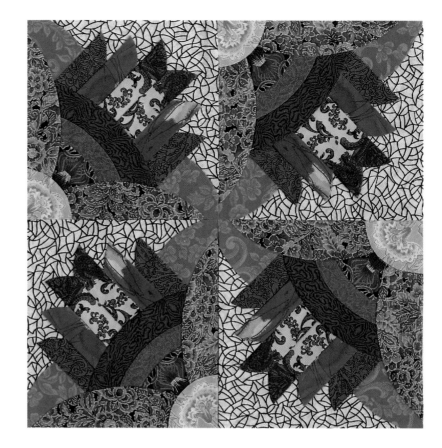

HOLLYHOCK

When my sister and I were growing up, my aunt gave us a small area of her garden to plant. We chose hollyhocks and poppies. Both grew very well, and during the summer the hollyhocks were taller than we could reach. One afternoon a swallowtail butterfly came by and took nectar from our flowers, and this made me so proud and happy.

The tall, slender hollyhock is native to China. Young children once made dolls with hollyhocks. They used buds for the head and petals, turned upside down, to make little dresses. In this block, I placed four very slender hollyhocks facing diagonally inward to create a symmetrical design.

INSTRUCTIONS
Templates on page 104.

To make the block, cut the required number of pieces indicated on the templates. To assemble the block, sew the pieces together in the following sequence, using the diagram as a guide.

1. Piece A is an 8½" (22cm) square. This includes seam allowance.
2. Lay out all placement templates on A and draw guidelines.
3. Appliqué B and C onto A.
4. Appliqué two D's onto No. 3.
5. Appliqué two E's onto No. 4.
6. Appliqué two F's onto No. 5.
7. Appliqué two G's onto No. 6.
8. Appliqué two H's onto No. 7.
9. Appliqué I onto No. 8.
10. Appliqué J, L, and N onto No. 9.
11. Appliqué K, M, and O onto No. 10.
12. Repeat the above steps to make four squares. Sew the squares together.

Finished block size: 16" × 16" (41cm × 41cm)

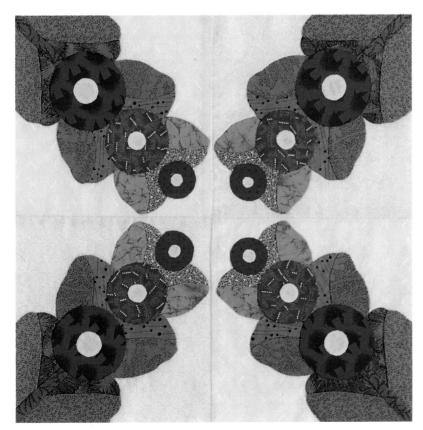

PARROT'S BEAK

This is an attractive but strange looking shrub from New Zealand. It has delicate foliage and pink flower blooms in a sickle-shape that resembles a parrot's beak. Here, the shape of the bird's beak is repeated throughout the block. The vibrantly colored half-circles are meant to suggest parrot faces.

INSTRUCTIONS
Templates on page 105.

To make the block, cut the required number of pieces indicated on the templates. To assemble the block, sew the pieces together in the following sequence, using the diagram as a guide.

1. Appliqué B and C onto A.
2. Appliqué D and E onto No. 1.
3. Appliqué F, G, H, and I onto No. 2.
4. Appliqué J, K, L, M, and N onto No. 3.
5. Repeat the above steps to make four squares. Sew the squares together.

Finished block size: 16" × 16" (41cm × 41cm)

SHAMROCK

One spring day my older sister took me and the neighbor children to a large green field. We picked armfuls of shamrock flowers, and soon we were wearing shamrock crowns and shamrock bracelets. I hope our happy young voices still echo over that beautiful field.

The shamrock is the national emblem of Ireland. The triple leaf signifies the Trinity and is associated with St. Patrick and the conversion of the Irish to Christianity. Finding a four-leaf clover means good luck in the Western tradition. In this block, I placed four shamrocks side by side to create heart-shaped forms in the center. This design offers many ways of connecting the blocks to create a continuous pattern.

INSTRUCTIONS
Templates on page 108.

To make one block, cut the required number of pieces indicated on the templates. Cutting instructions for making a quilt, and assembly instructions for making a block or a quilt are given on the following pages.

Finished block size: 16" × 16" (41cm × 41cm)

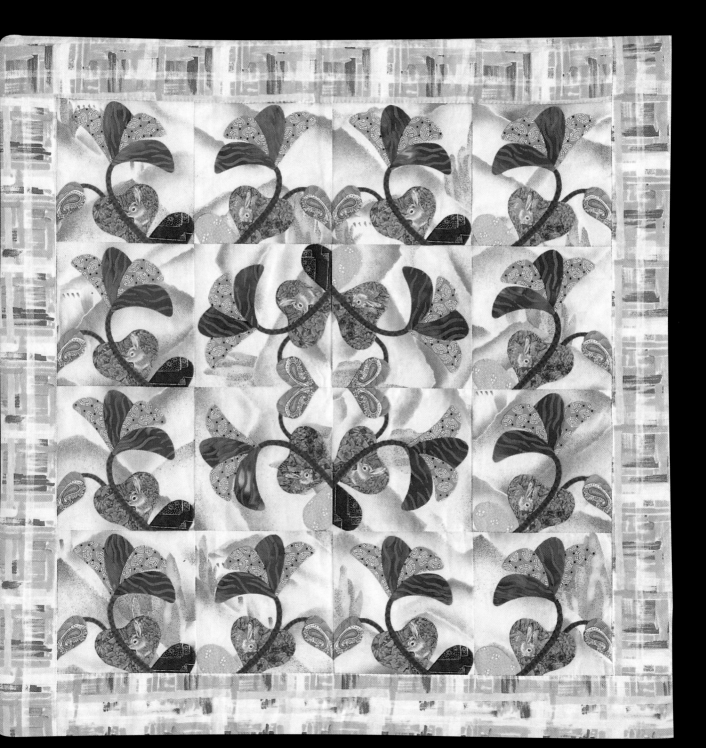

SHAMROCK: *Quilt*

	WALL/CRIB	TWIN	DOUBLE/QUEEN	KING
Size (inches)	39 × 39	71 × 87	87 × 87	103 × 103
Size (centimeters)	99 × 99	180 × 221	221 × 221	262 × 262
Setting	4 × 4	8 × 10	10 × 10	12 × 12
Quarter blocks	16	80	100	144

Fabric needed: *Yards (centimeters) for 45" (114cm) fabric*

Template A	¾ (69)	3⅝ (331)	4½ (411)	6½ (594)
Template B	⅛ (11)	½ (46)	⅝ (57)	⅞ (80)
Template C	⅛ (11)	¼ (23)	⅜ (34)	½ (46)
Template D	⅛ (11)	¼ (23)	⅜ (34)	½ (46)
Template E	⅛ (11)	½ (46)	½ (46)	¾ (69)
Template F	¼ (23)	1⅛ (103)	1½ (137)	2 (183)
Template G	⅛ (11)	½ (46)	½ (46)	⅝ (57)
Template H	⅜ (34)	¾ (69)	1 (91)	1¼ (114)
Template I	⅛ (11)	⅝ (57)	¾ (69)	1 (91)
Template J	⅛ (11)	⅝ (57)	¾ (69)	1 (91)
Template K	⅜ (34)	1½ (137)	1⅞ (171)	2¾ (251)
Border	¾ (69)	2½ (229)	2½ (229)	3 (274)

Cutting

Template A	16	80	100	144
Template B	16	80	100	144
Template C	16	80	100	144
Template D	16	80	100	144
Template E	16	80	100	144
Template F	16	80	100	144
Template G	16	80	100	144
Template H	16	80	100	144
Template I	16	80	100	144
Template J	16	80	100	144
Template K	16	80	100	144

Border width is 4" (10cm) including ¼" (6mm) seam allowance.

3.

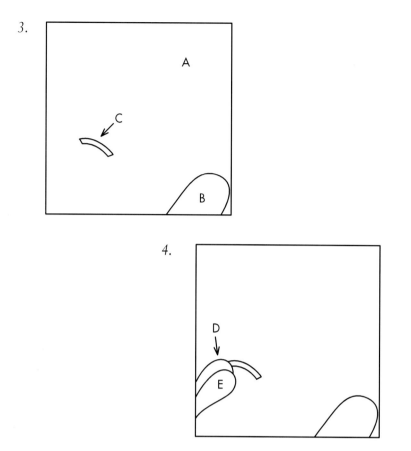

ASSEMBLY INSTRUCTIONS

To assemble each block, sew the pieces together in the following sequence, using the step-by-step drawings and the diagram as guides.

1. Piece A is an 8½" (22cm) square. This includes seam allowance.
2. Lay out all placement templates on A and draw guidelines.
3. Appliqué C and B onto A.
4. Appliqué D and E onto No. 3.
5. Appliqué F onto No. 4.
6. Appliqué G onto No. 5.
7. Appliqué H, I, J, and K onto No. 6.
8. Repeat the above steps to make four squares (quarter blocks). Sew the squares together.

In the quilt shown, the squares (quarter blocks) have been turned, creating a fragmented overall pattern. To make this quilt, assemble and sew together the number of quarter blocks required to complete your project. For example, the quilt shown here is wall hanging size with sixteen quarter blocks sewn together in four rows of four plus a border.

4.

5.

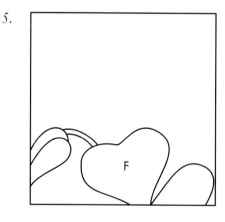

6.

7.

MANDEVILLA

At one point my family moved from the mountains to a new home by the sea. While walking along the street between the train station and our house, I would see mandevillas every day. I met a very handsome boy at my new school, and I later found out that those flowers were growing in front of his house.

Mandevilla "Alice du Pont" are tropical vines grown throughout the year in the warmest parts of the United States. In this block, I divided the back-ground into four triangles to emphasize the activities going on between the flowers and the vines; I also used several different colors to impart the feeling of movement.

INSTRUCTIONS
Templates on page 109.

To make the block, cut the required number of pieces indicated on the templates. To assemble the block, sew the pieces together in the following sequence, using the diagram as a guide.

1. To make four A pieces, cut a 19½" (50cm) square into four equal triangles; this includes seam allowance.
2. Lay out all placement templates on A and draw guidelines.
3. Appliqué B onto A.
4. Appliqué C onto No. 3.
5. Appliqué D onto No. 4.
6. Appliqué F and G onto No. 5.
7. Appliqué E and H onto No. 6.
8. Repeat the above steps to make four triangles. Sew the triangles together.

Finished block size: 16" × 16" (41cm × 41cm)

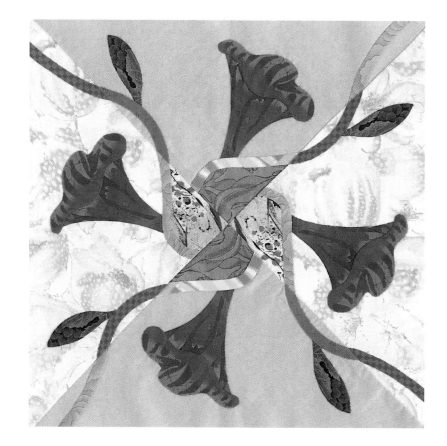

MAGIC FLOWER OF THE INCAS

This interesting evergreen shrub with a long tubular corolla is little known in the United States. It originated in the Andes, where young Indian girls used the flower to adorn themselves for religious ceremonies. The background fabric of this design symbolizes the clear blue sky of the Andes. I placed the flowers in a way that suggests movement in the pattern.

INSTRUCTIONS
Templates on page 110.

To make the block, cut the required number of pieces indicated on the templates. To assemble the block, sew the pieces together in the following sequence, using the diagram as a guide.

1. Piece A is an 8½" (22cm) square. This includes seam allowance.
2. Lay out all placement templates on A and draw guidelines.
3. Appliqué B and C onto A.
4. Appliqué two G's onto No. 3.
5. Appliqué two D's onto No. 4.
6. Appliqué two E's onto No. 5.
7. Appliqué F onto No. 6.
8. Repeat the above steps to make four squares. Sew the squares together.

Finished block size: 16" × 16" (41cm × 41cm)

GOLDEN COIN

One summer, my sister, my brother, and I went on a little field trip to catch insects. We didn't have much luck. I remember the three of us sitting on a bamboo bench eating watermelon, and right behind us were many golden coin flowers. I couldn't help thinking about how quickly the summer had gone by.

We find this particular bush growing in abundance in Japan where, because of its brilliant yellow color, it is called the golden coin. Therefore, I used rich shades of yellow and orange to symbolize this flower. Many variations of blue and violet on the leaves compliment the golden hues.

INSTRUCTIONS
Templates on page 111.

To make the block, cut the required number of pieces indicated on the templates. To assemble the block, sew the pieces together in the following sequence, using the diagram as a guide.

1. Piece A is a 16½" (42cm) square. This includes seam allowance.
2. Lay out all placement templates on A and draw guidelines.
3. In one corner, appliqué two B's onto A.
4. Appliqué C onto No. 3.
5. Appliqué two D's onto No. 4.
6. Appliqué two E's onto No. 5.
7. Appliqué F onto No. 6.
8. Appliqué two G's onto No. 7.
9. Appliqué two H's onto No. 8.
10. Appliqué two I's onto No. 9.
11. Repeat the above steps in each of the remaining corners of the background square.

Finished block size: 16" × 16" (41cm × 41cm)

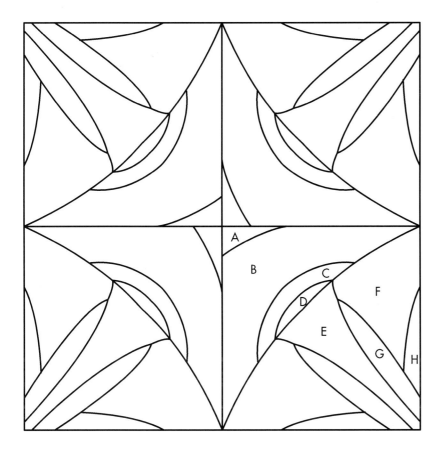

ANGEL TRUMPET

A long time ago, one of my older sisters returned from South America, and in her photo album I found a picture of an unusual flower. It was an angel trumpet, and today whenever I see this flower, it invites me to visit her magical wonderland.

The tube-shaped white, light pink, and light orange flowers truly resemble angel's trumpets. They usually start to bloom in the evening and emit a sweet fragrance. In this block design, the four-pointed center motif represents an early evening star.

INSTRUCTIONS
Templates on page 113.

To make one block, cut the required number of pieces indicated on the templates. Cutting instructions for making a quilt, and assembly instructions for making a block or a quilt are given on the following pages.

Finished block size: 16" × 16" (41cm × 41cm)

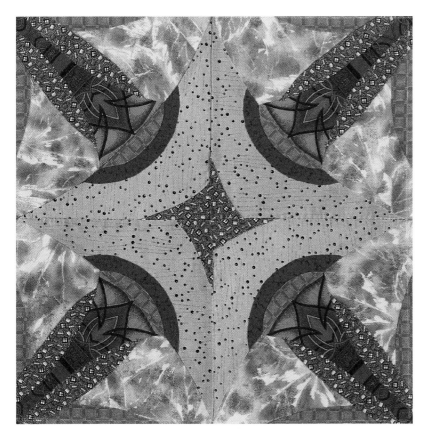

ANGEL TRUMPET: *Quilt*

WALL/CRIB	
Size (inches)	40 × 56
Size (centimeters)	102 × 142
Setting	4 × 6
Quarter blocks	12
Variation square I	4
Variation square II	8

Variation square I

Fabric needed: Yards (centimeters) for 45" (114cm) fabric

Template A	⅛ (11)
Template B	½ (46)
Template C	⅛ (11)
Template D	⅛ (11)
Template E	⅜ (34)
Template F	¼ (23)
Template G	½ (46)
Template H	¾ (69)
Variation square I: assorted colors	½ (46)
Variation square II	¾ (69)
Additional template A	¼ (23)
First border	¼ (23)
Second border	1¾ (160)

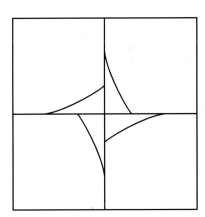

Variation square II

Cutting

Template A	12
Template B	12
Template C	12
Template D	12
Template E	24
Template F	24
Template G	24
Template H	24
Variation square I: 4½" (11cm) square	16
Variation square II: 4½" (11cm) square	32
Additional template A	32

First border width is 1½" (4cm) including ¼" (6mm) seam allowance.

Second border width is 3½" (9cm) including ¼" (6mm) seam allowance.

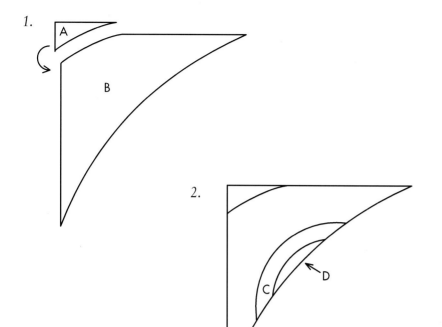

1.

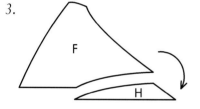

3.

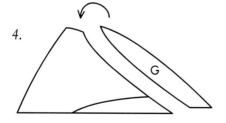

4.

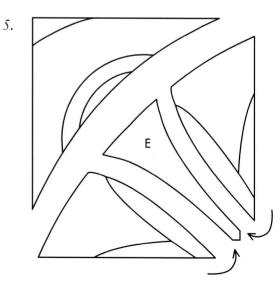

5.

To assemble each block, sew the pieces together in the following sequence, using the step-by-step drawings and the diagram as guides.

1. Appliqué A onto B.
2. Appliqué C and D onto No. 1.
3. Appliqué H onto F and repeat.
4. Appliqué G onto a No. 3 and repeat.
5. Appliqué E between the two No. 4's and sew to No. 2.
6. Repeat the above steps to make four squares (quarter blocks). Sew the squares together.

To make this quilt, quarter blocks are combined with two variation squares. Assemble and sew together the required number of each. Using the diagram as a placement guide, sew six rows of four squares and add two borders.

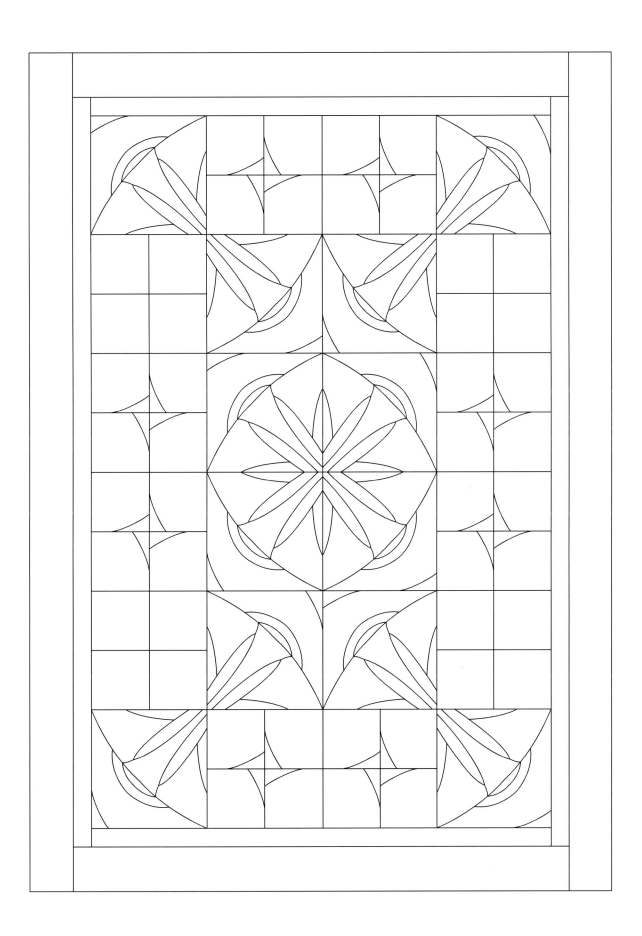

CYCLAMEN

My sisters and I sometimes looked for natural herbs growing in the hills near our home. One autumn I found a beautiful pink flower that I later learned was a cyclamen. I wanted to take the plant with me and tried to dig it up, but the roots were too long and deep. I still feel sorrow when I think that I disturbed this flower by trying to take it home.

When the air turns crisp and we are busy preparing Christmas presents for loved ones, beautiful cyclamen is displayed in shop windows and on many street corners. In this block, I have planted my purple cyclamen on two shades of background fabric to obtain more depth in the design. A touch of pink in the leaves balances the brilliance of the flowers.

INSTRUCTIONS
Templates on page 115.

To make the block, cut the required number of pieces indicated on the templates. To assemble the block, sew the pieces together in the following sequence, using the diagram as a guide.

1. Piece A is an 8½" (22cm) square. This includes seam allowance.
2. Lay out all placement templates on A and draw guidelines.
3. Appliqué D onto A.
4. Appliqué B and F onto No. 3.
5. Appliqué C and E onto No. 4.
6. Appliqué G and H onto No. 5.
7. Appliqué I and J onto No. 6.
8. Appliqué K and L onto No. 7.
9. Appliqué M onto No. 8.
10. Appliqué N onto No. 9.
11. Repeat the above steps to make four squares. Sew the squares together.

Finished block size: 16" × 16" (41cm × 41cm)

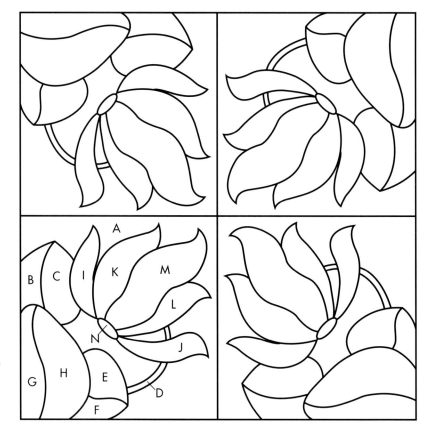

GLADIOLUS

The summer when I was nine years old, I had to stay at my aunt's home, without the rest of my family. I saw one of my neighbor friends talking with his mother while they sat under a pear tree. I turned back to my aunt's garden filled with many gladiolus flowers, but still I felt very lonely.

Gladiolus are very showy, highly decorative flowers that have been hybridized in a wide range of colors, including lime green and deep red-purple. In this block, I placed individual flowers and leaves at the four corners with another single flower in the center.

INSTRUCTIONS
Templates on page 117.

To make the block, cut the required number of pieces indicated on the templates. To assemble the block, sew the pieces together in the following sequence, using the diagram as a guide.

1. Piece A is an 8½" (22cm) square. This includes seam allowance.
2. Lay out all placement templates on A and draw guidelines.
3. Appliqué B and C onto A.
4. Appliqué D onto No. 3.
5. Appliqué two E's onto No. 4.
6. Appliqué F onto No. 5.
7. Appliqué two G's onto No. 6.
8. Appliqué six H's onto No. 7.
9. Appliqué two I's onto No. 8.
10. Repeat the above steps to make four squares. Sew the squares together.

Finished block size: 16" × 16" (41cm × 41cm)

ROSE

The rose is the symbol of love, beauty, and sentiment. To early Christians it was the emblem of the church. Ancient Egyptians grew roses to carpet Cleopatra's floors and cover her tables when she entertained Mark Anthony. Today, oil from rose petals is used in scenting cosmetics; to procure one ounce of pure oil requires 60,000 roses. Here, I created a stylized rose in purple, red, and orange with blue-green leaves. The blue-purple heart shape in the center of each motif symbolizes the romance of roses.

INSTRUCTIONS
Templates on page 118.

To make the block, cut the required number of pieces indicated on the templates. To assemble the block, sew the pieces together in the following sequence, using the diagram as a guide.

1. Piece A is a 16½" (42cm) square. This includes seam allowance.
2. Lay out all placement templates on A and draw guidelines.
3. In one corner, appliqué B onto A.
4. Appliqué C onto No. 3.
5. Appliqué D, E, F, and G onto No. 4.
6. Appliqué two H's onto No. 5.
7. Appliqué two I's onto No. 6.
8. Appliqué two J's onto No. 7.
9. Appliqué two K's onto No. 8.
10. Repeat the above steps in each of the remaining corners of the background square.

Finished block size: 16" × 16" (41cm × 41cm)

EVERGREEN MAGNOLIA

泰山木

Near our home by the sea, we planted a magnolia tree that bloomed beautifully every year. It was the only one of its kind in the neighborhood, and I was very proud of it. The petals would drift down into the small pond under the tree, and to me they looked like small boats sailing in a lake.

In this magnolia design, I used a bluish white square for the background. It implies a pleasant, clear, spring sky and adds a dramatic effect. Surrounding it are intense blue-green leaves and brilliant magenta-red flowers.

INSTRUCTIONS
Templates on page 120.

To make the block, cut the required number of pieces indicated on the templates. To assemble the block, sew the pieces together in the following sequence, using the diagram as a guide.

1. Piece A is a 16½" (42cm) square. This includes seam allowance.
2. Lay out all placement templates on A and draw guidelines.
3. In one corner, appliqué B onto A.
4. Appliqué C and D onto No. 3.
5. Appliqué E onto No. 4.
6. Appliqué G and F onto No. 5.
7. Appliqué two I's onto No. 6.
8. Appliqué two J's onto No. 7.
9. Sew two K's together along the straight edge, then open the seam and appliqué onto No. 8.
10. Appliqué H onto No. 9.
11. Repeat the above steps in each of the remaining corners of the background square.

Finished block size: 16" × 16" (41cm × 41cm)

IRIS

May 5th is boys' day in Japan. One of the customs we followed during this week was to collect iris roots and stems. These were placed in hot bath water, or used to decorate the roof. This custom symbolizes keeping the family healthy during the coming year.

Because he believed it was the flower of eloquence, the King of Egypt, Thutmose III, brought the iris from Syria in the second millennium B.C. to place on the brow of the silent Sphinx. In Greek mythology, Iris was admired as the goddess of the rainbow. In this block, I chose to arrange irises with rainbow colors to represent the Greek goddess.

INSTRUCTIONS
Templates on page 122.

To make the block, cut the required number of pieces indicated on the templates. To assemble the block, sew the pieces together in the following sequence, using the diagram as a guide.

1. Piece A is an 8½" (22cm) square. This includes seam allowance.
2. Lay out all placement templates on A and draw guidelines.
3. Appliqué B and C onto A.
4. Appliqué D and E onto No. 3.
5. Appliqué F onto No. 4.
6. Appliqué G onto No. 5.
7. Appliqué I, H, and J onto No. 6.
8. Appliqué K and L onto No. 7.
9. Appliqué M, N, and O onto No. 8.
10. Repeat the above steps to make four squares. Sew the squares together.

Finished block size: 16" × 16" (41cm × 41cm)

CHERRY BLOSSOM

Every time I see cherry blossoms I remember high school. The street leading to our school was lined with long rows of cherry trees. One warm sunny day, while I walked to class with several of my friends, cherry blossom petals fell on our heads like snow. We took a snapshot of this wonderful event.

This flower is the emblem of femininity in China and is the national symbol of Japan. Springtime in Japan is unthinkable without cherry blossoms. This design is meant to feel like sixteenth-century Japan. A single cherry blossom floats in the center of the hazy spring sky. Several layers of petals form fan-shaped blossoms at each corner, and whimsical blue leaves at both sides express cherry blossoms in full bloom in early spring.

INSTRUCTIONS
Templates on page 124.

To make one block, cut the required number of pieces indicated on the templates. Cutting instructions for making a quilt, and assembly instructions for making a block or a quilt are given on the following pages.

Finished block size: 16" × 16" (41cm × 41cm)

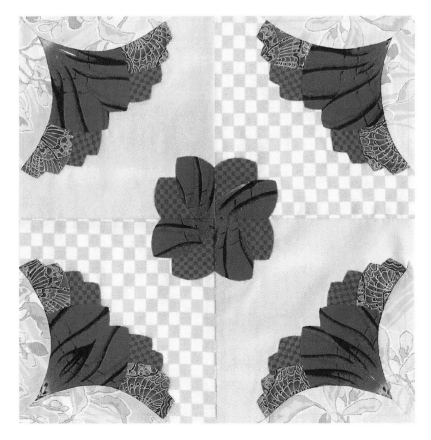

CHERRY BLOSSOM: *Quilt*

	WALL/CRIB

Size (inches)	42 × 50
Size (centimeters)	107 × 127
Setting	4 × 5
Quarter blocks	17
Checkerboard quarter blocks	3

Fabric needed: Yards (centimeters) for 45" (114cm) fabric

Template A	⅞ (80)
Template B	¼ (23)
Template C	¼ (23)
Template D	½ (46)
Template E	½ (46)

(Note: Templates F and G are not used in the quilt.)

Checkerboard square (light)	½ (46) — *includes border*
Checkerboard square (dark)	½ (46) — *includes border*
First border	¼ (23)
Second border	¼ (23)
Third border	1½ (137)

Checkerboard quarter block

Cutting

Template A	17
Template B	34
Template C	34
Template D	34
Template E	34

Checkerboard square (light): 2½" (6cm) square	40	— *includes border*
Checkerboard square (dark): 2½" (6cm) square	40	— *includes border*

First border width is 1½" (4cm) including ¼" (6mm) seam allowance, piece if desired.
Second border width is 1½" (4cm) including ¼" (6mm) seam allowance.
Third border width is 5" (13cm) including ¼" (6mm) seam allowance.

3.

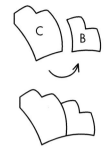

4.

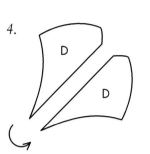

5.

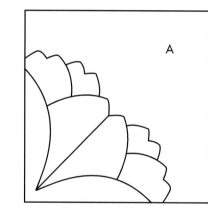

6.

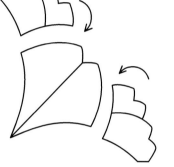

7.

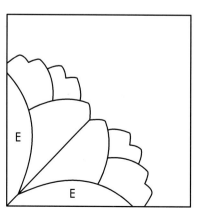

8.

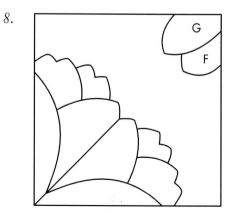

To assemble each block, sew the pieces together in the following sequence, using the step-by-step drawings and the diagram as guides.

1. Piece A is an 8½" (22cm) square. This includes seam allowance.
2. Lay out all placement templates on A and draw guidelines.
3. Sew B and C together; repeat.
4. Sew two D's together along the straight edge and open the seam.
5. Appliqué two No. 3's to No. 4.
6. Appliqué No. 5 to piece A.
7. Appliqué two E's onto No. 6.
8. Appliqué F and G onto No. 7.
9. Repeat the above steps to make four squares (quarter blocks). Sew the squares together.

To make this quilt, quarter blocks are combined with checkerboard quarter blocks. Assemble and sew together the required number of each. Note that templates F and G are not needed for the quilt. Using the diagram as a placement guide, sew five rows of four squares and add the pieced borders.

TEMPLATES

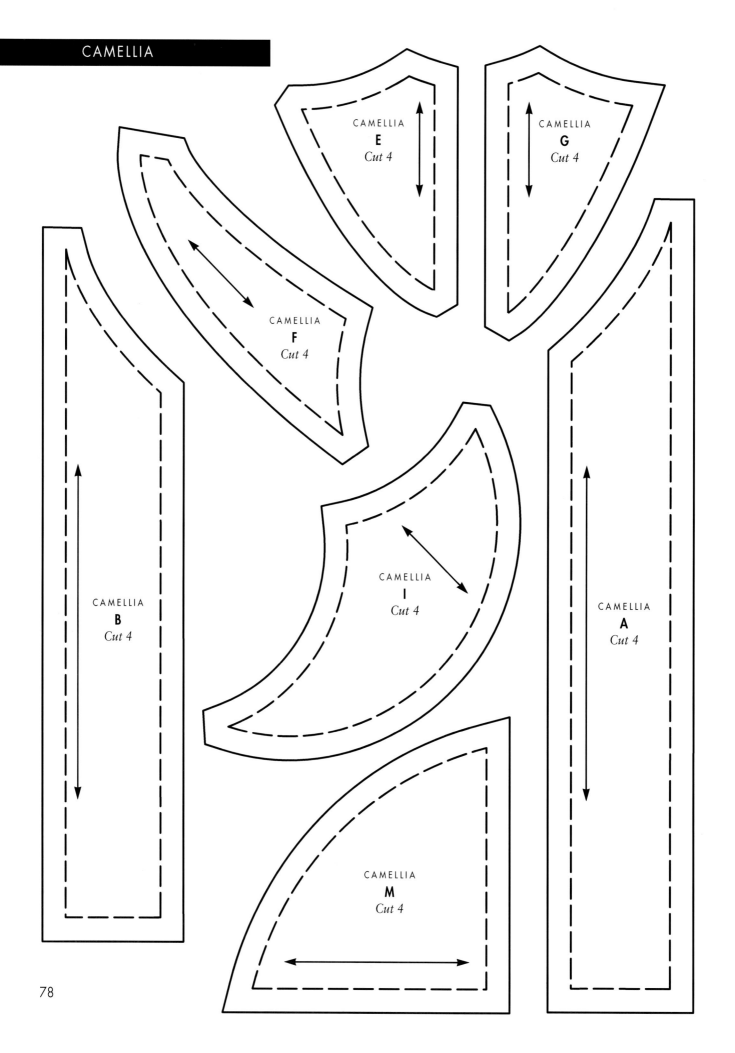

CAMELLIA
E
Cut 4

CAMELLIA
G
Cut 4

CAMELLIA
F
Cut 4

CAMELLIA
B
Cut 4

CAMELLIA
I
Cut 4

CAMELLIA
A
Cut 4

CAMELLIA
M
Cut 4

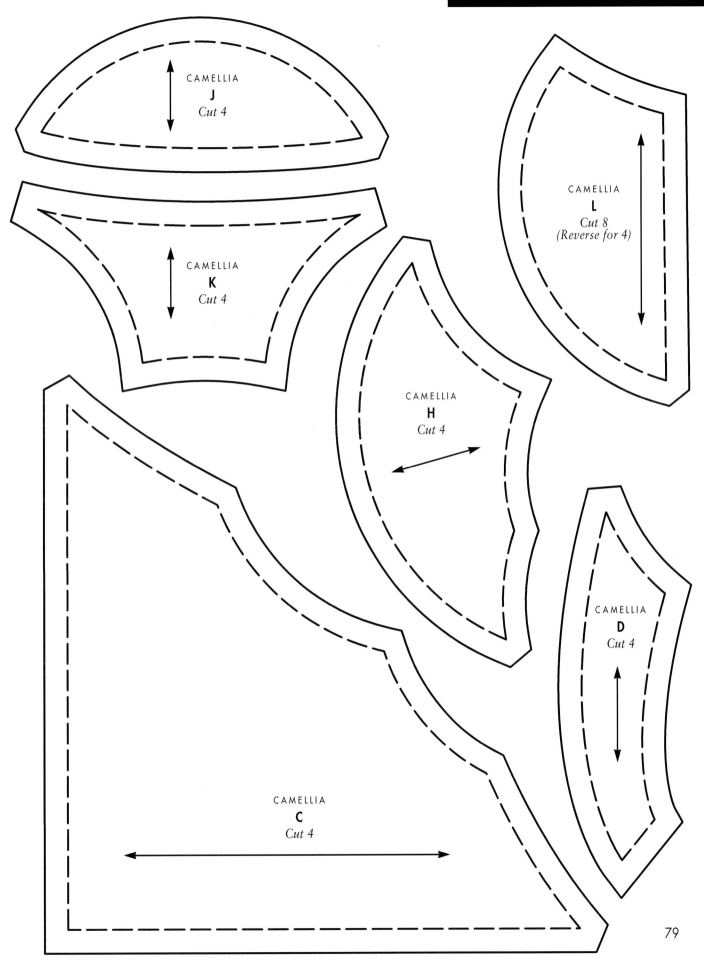

CAMELLIA
J
Cut 4

CAMELLIA
K
Cut 4

CAMELLIA
L
Cut 8
(Reverse for 4)

CAMELLIA
H
Cut 4

CAMELLIA
D
Cut 4

CAMELLIA
C
Cut 4

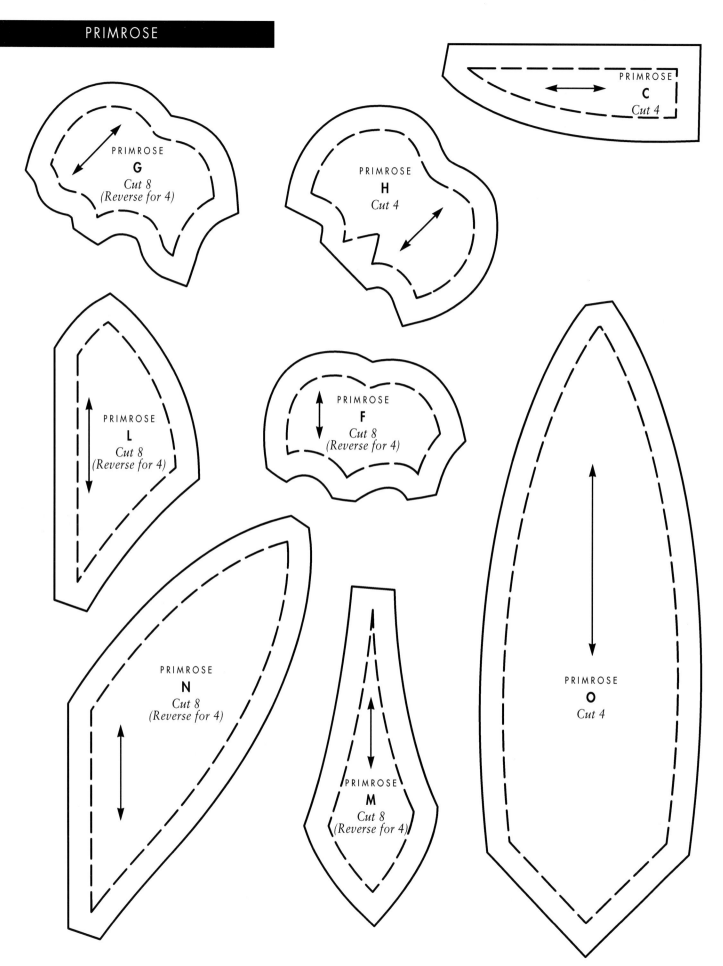

PRIMROSE
C
Cut 4

PRIMROSE
G
Cut 8
(Reverse for 4)

PRIMROSE
H
Cut 4

PRIMROSE
L
Cut 8
(Reverse for 4)

PRIMROSE
F
Cut 8
(Reverse for 4)

PRIMROSE
N
Cut 8
(Reverse for 4)

PRIMROSE
M
Cut 8
(Reverse for 4)

PRIMROSE
O
Cut 4

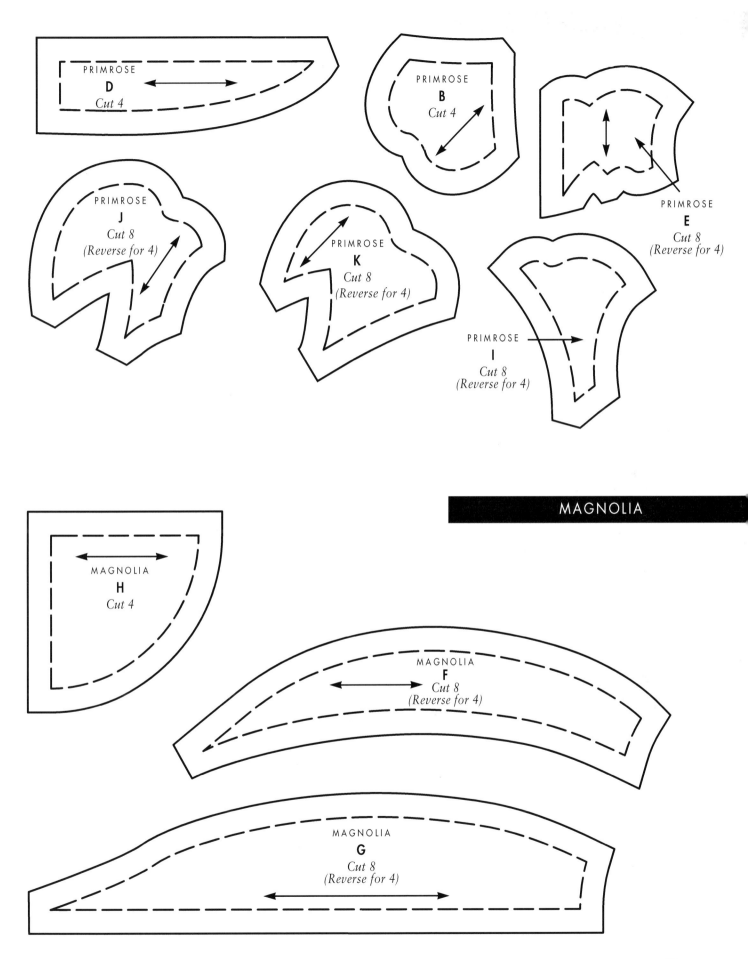

PRIMROSE
D
Cut 4

PRIMROSE
B
Cut 4

PRIMROSE
E
Cut 8
(Reverse for 4)

PRIMROSE
J
Cut 8
(Reverse for 4)

PRIMROSE
K
Cut 8
(Reverse for 4)

PRIMROSE
I
Cut 8
(Reverse for 4)

MAGNOLIA

MAGNOLIA
H
Cut 4

MAGNOLIA
F
Cut 8
(Reverse for 4)

MAGNOLIA
G
Cut 8
(Reverse for 4)

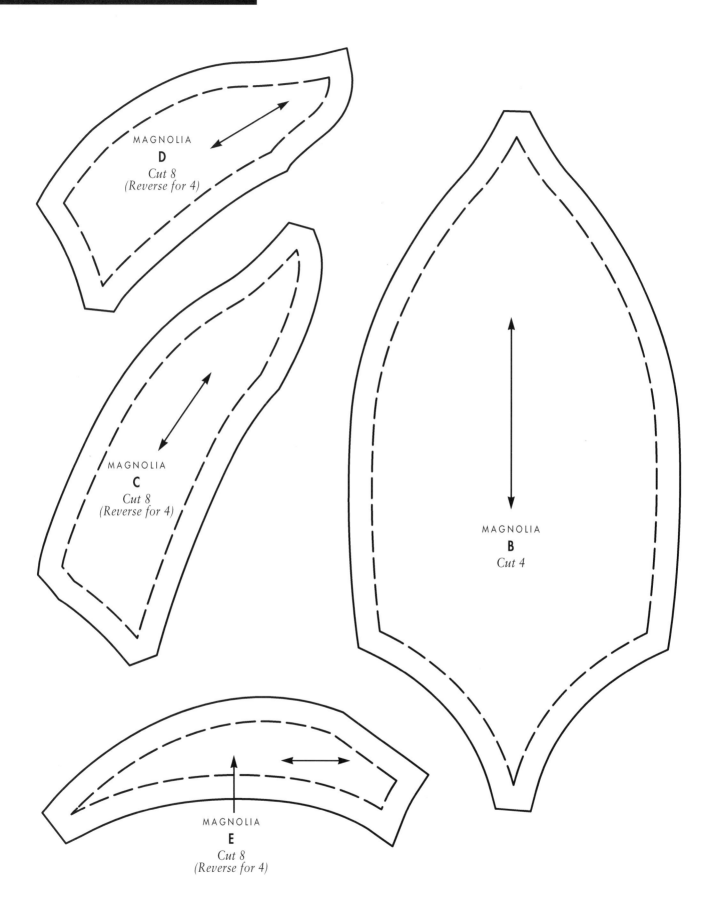

MAGNOLIA
D
Cut 8
(Reverse for 4)

MAGNOLIA
C
Cut 8
(Reverse for 4)

MAGNOLIA
B
Cut 4

MAGNOLIA
E
Cut 8
(Reverse for 4)

NOTE: The templates indicate the number of pieces needed for making one block. To determine the number of pieces needed to make a complete quilt, refer to the cutting charts that accompany the quilt instructions.

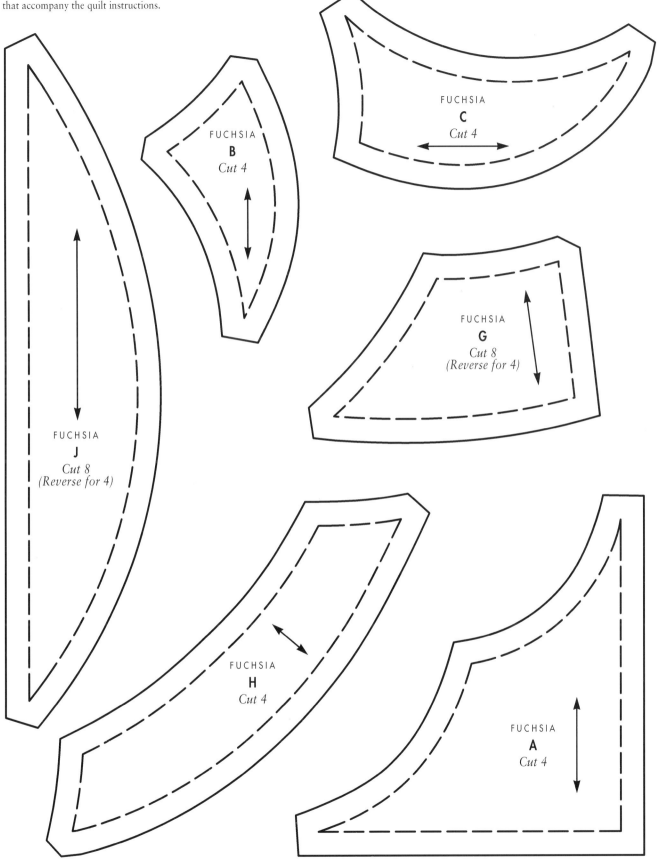

FUCHSIA
B
Cut 4

FUCHSIA
C
Cut 4

FUCHSIA
G
Cut 8
(Reverse for 4)

FUCHSIA
J
Cut 8
(Reverse for 4)

FUCHSIA
H
Cut 4

FUCHSIA
A
Cut 4

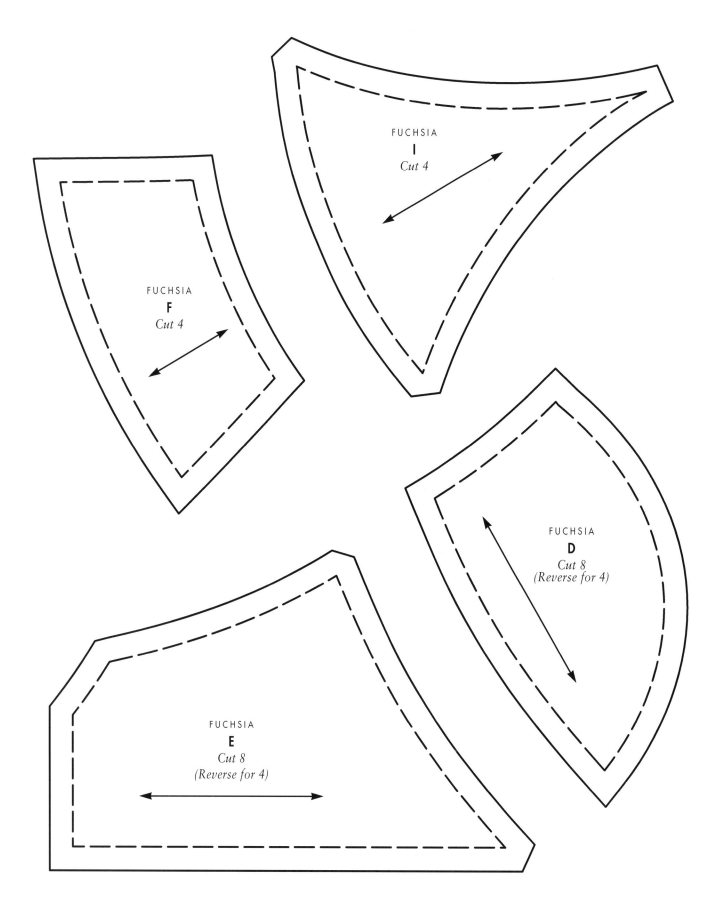

FUCHSIA
I
Cut 4

FUCHSIA
F
Cut 4

FUCHSIA
D
Cut 8
(Reverse for 4)

FUCHSIA
E
Cut 8
(Reverse for 4)

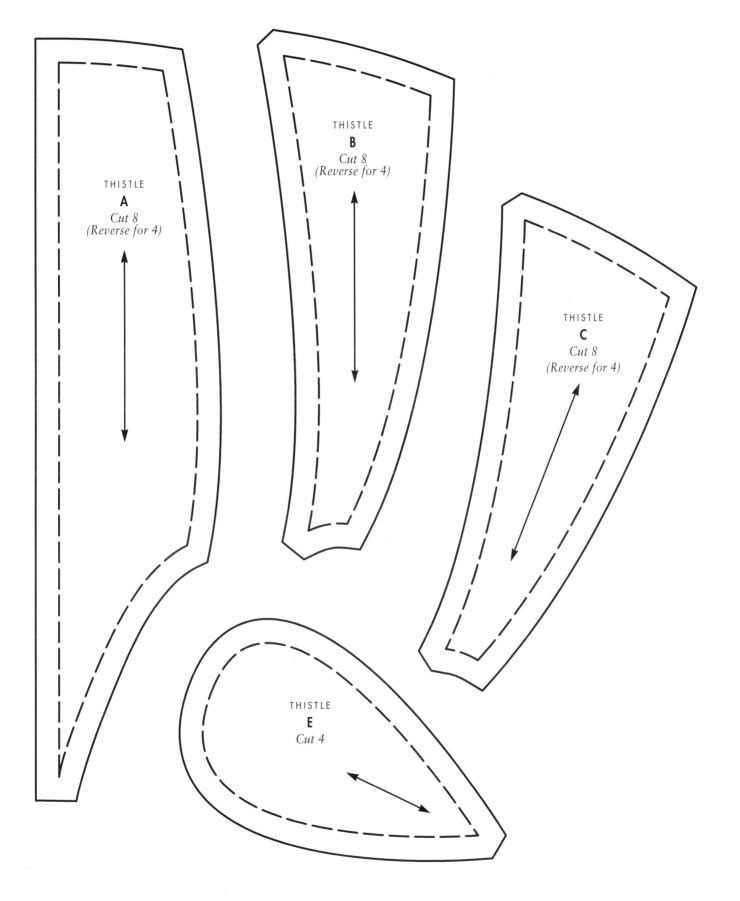

THISTLE
A
*Cut 8
(Reverse for 4)*

THISTLE
B
*Cut 8
(Reverse for 4)*

THISTLE
C
*Cut 8
(Reverse for 4)*

THISTLE
E
Cut 4

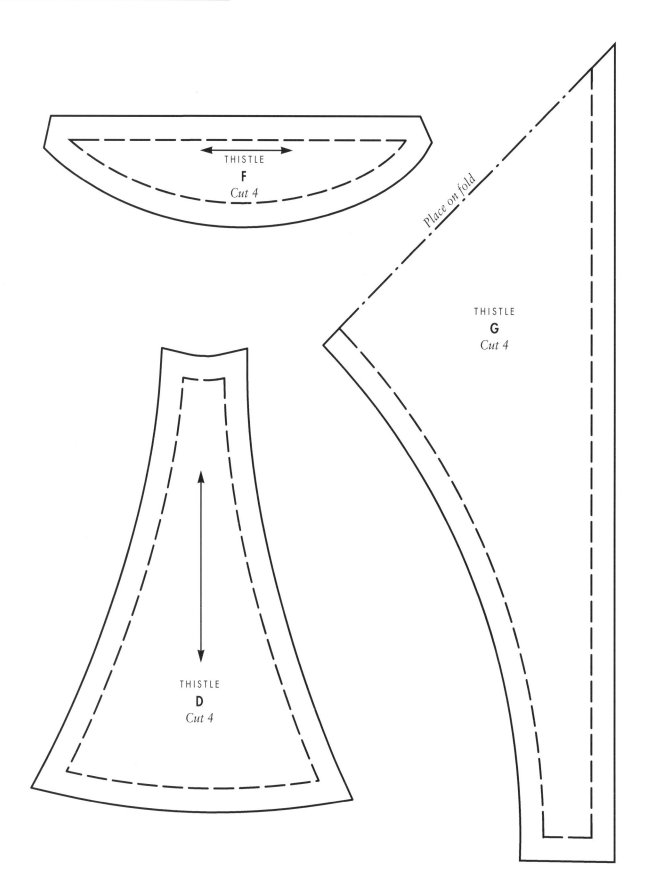

THISTLE
F
Cut 4

THISTLE
G
Cut 4

Place on fold

THISTLE
D
Cut 4

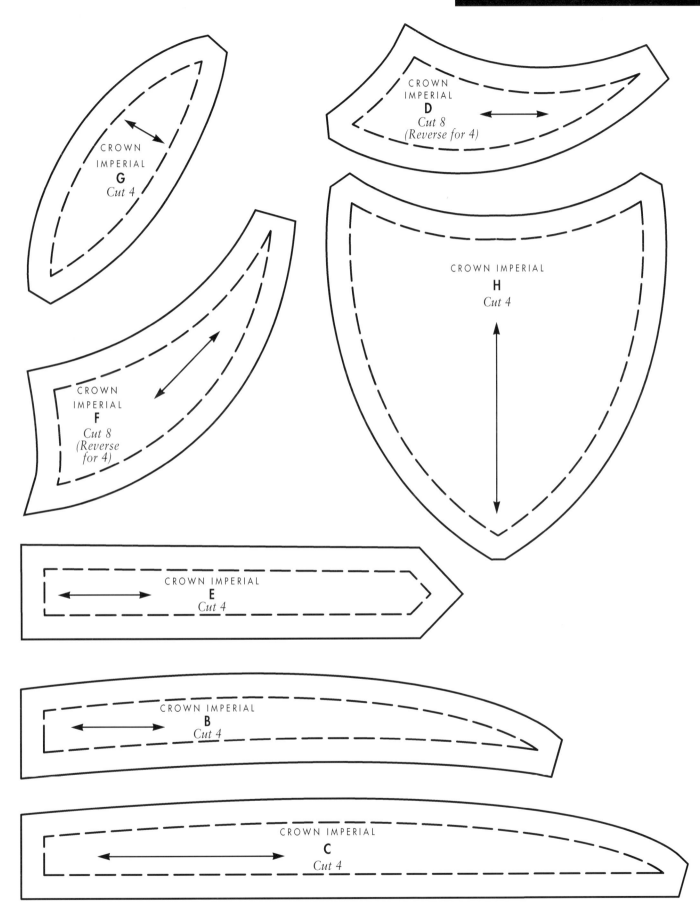

CROWN
IMPERIAL
G
Cut 4

CROWN
IMPERIAL
D
Cut 8
(Reverse for 4)

CROWN IMPERIAL
H
Cut 4

CROWN
IMPERIAL
F
Cut 8
(Reverse
for 4)

CROWN IMPERIAL
E
Cut 4

CROWN IMPERIAL
B
Cut 4

CROWN IMPERIAL
C
Cut 4

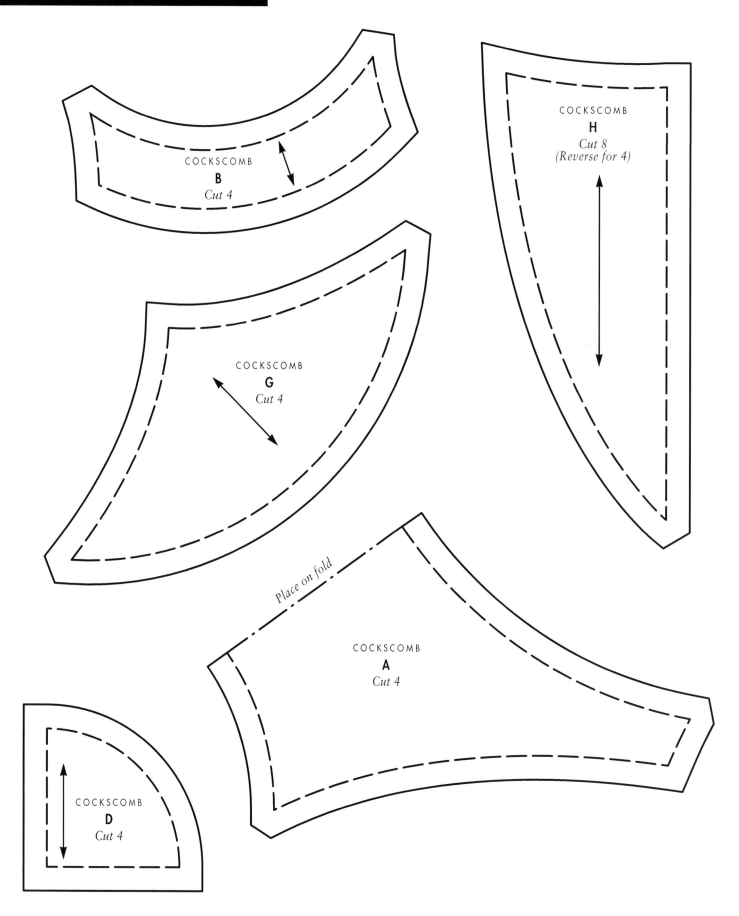

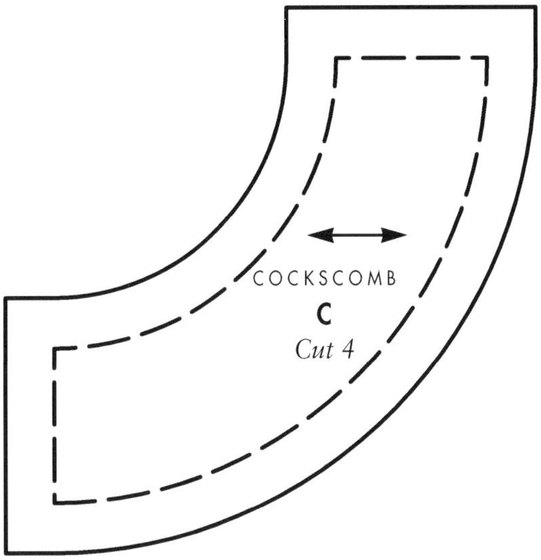

COCKSCOMB
C
Cut 4

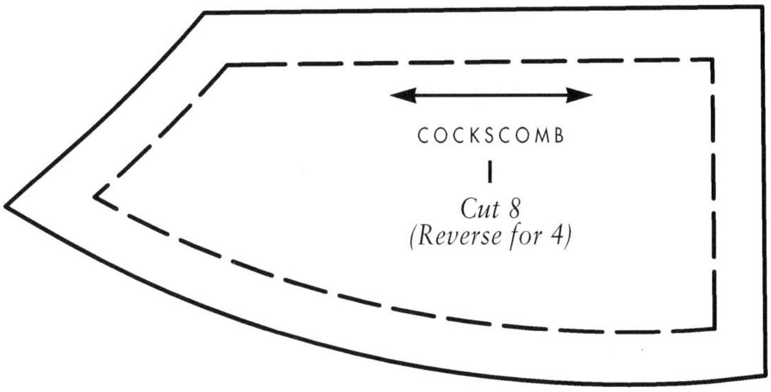

COCKSCOMB
I
Cut 8
(Reverse for 4)

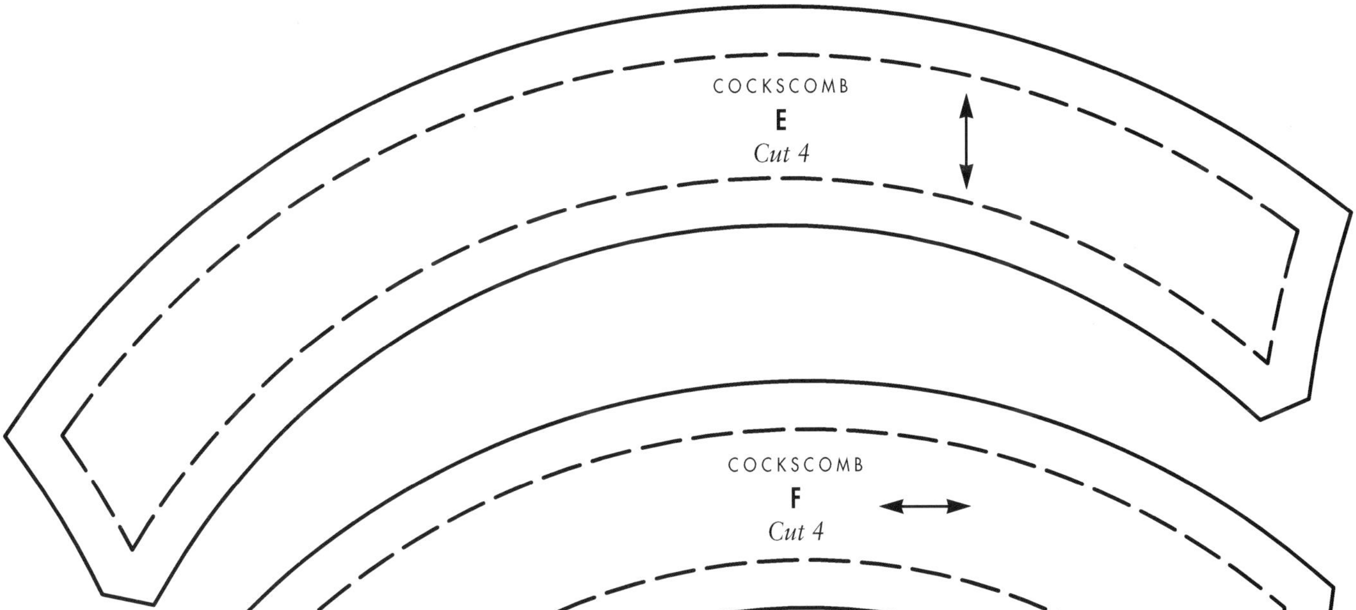

COCKSCOMB
E
Cut 4

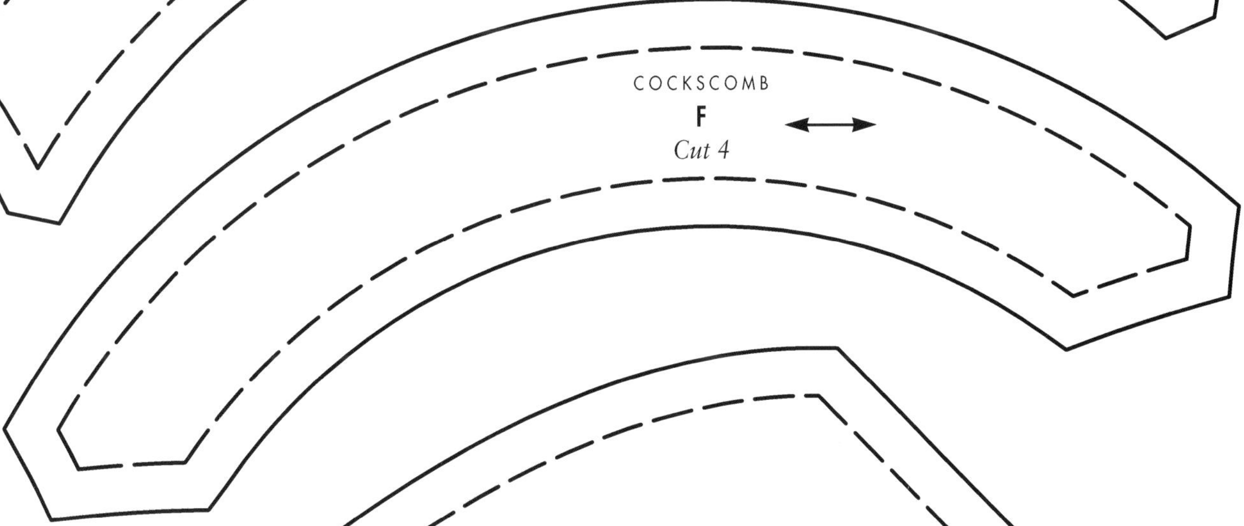

COCKSCOMB
F
Cut 4

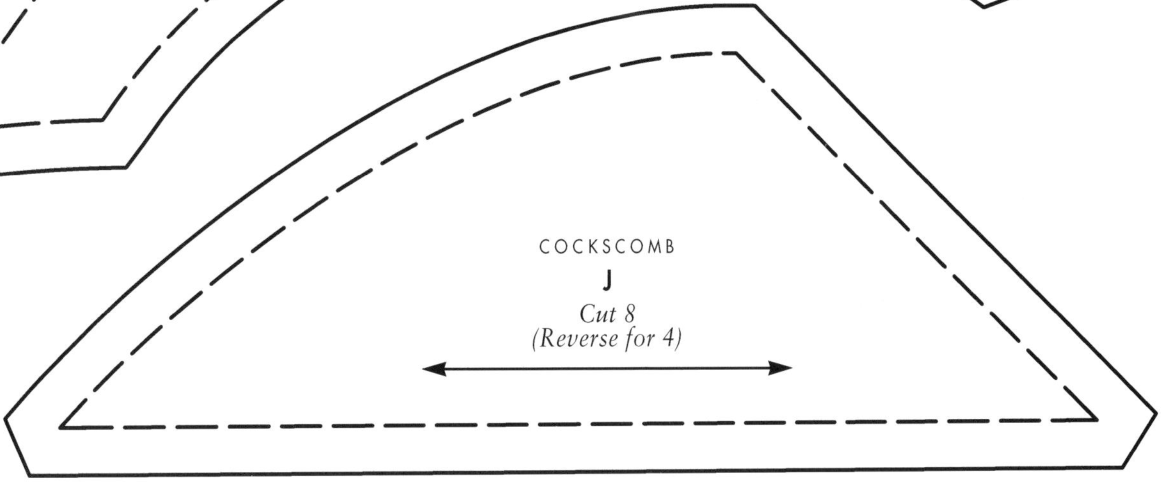

COCKSCOMB
J
Cut 8
(Reverse for 4)

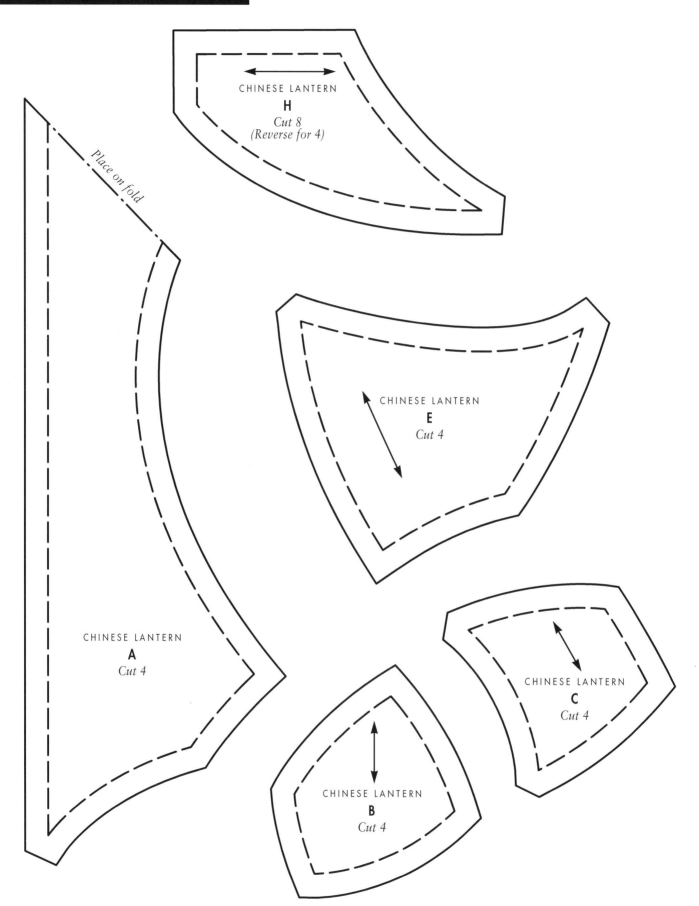

CHINESE LANTERN
H
Cut 8
(Reverse for 4)

CHINESE LANTERN
E
Cut 4

Place on fold

CHINESE LANTERN
A
Cut 4

CHINESE LANTERN
C
Cut 4

CHINESE LANTERN
B
Cut 4

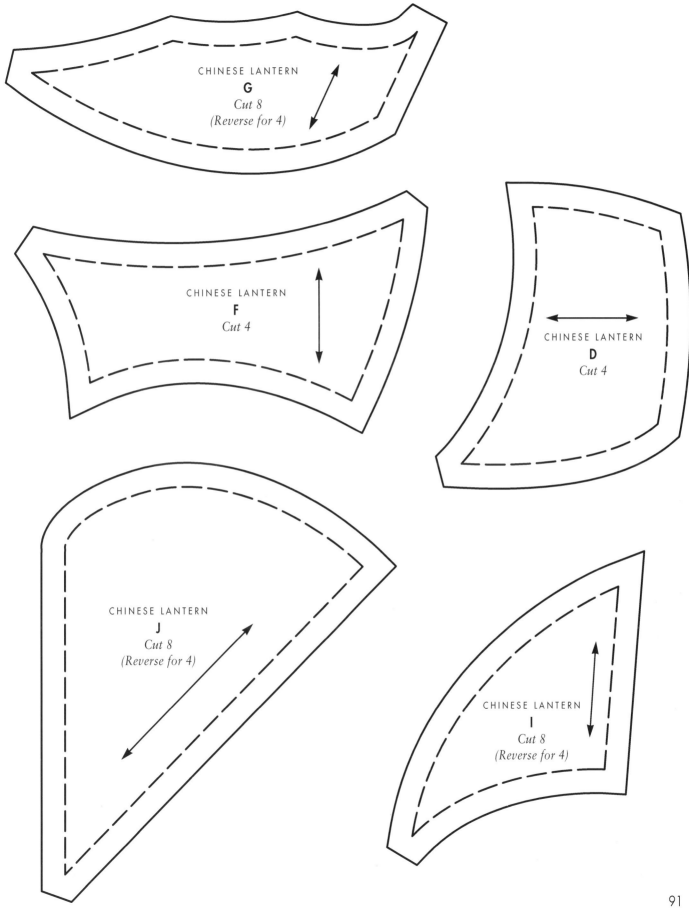

CHINESE LANTERN
G
Cut 8
(Reverse for 4)

CHINESE LANTERN
F
Cut 4

CHINESE LANTERN
D
Cut 4

CHINESE LANTERN
J
Cut 8
(Reverse for 4)

CHINESE LANTERN
I
Cut 8
(Reverse for 4)

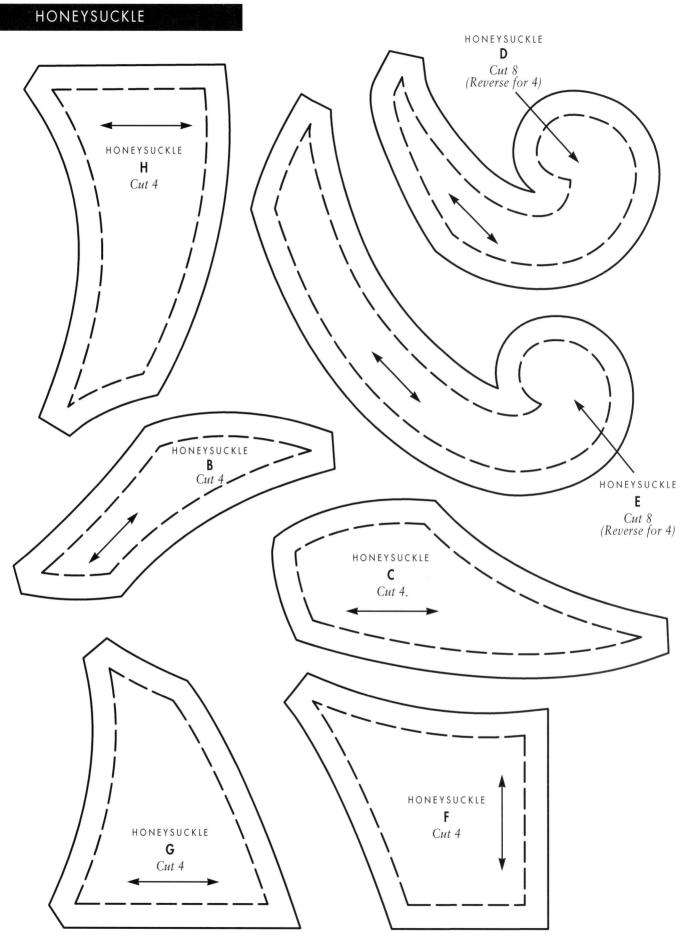

HONEYSUCKLE
D
*Cut 8
(Reverse for 4)*

HONEYSUCKLE
H
Cut 4

HONEYSUCKLE
B
Cut 4

HONEYSUCKLE
E
*Cut 8
(Reverse for 4)*

HONEYSUCKLE
C
Cut 4.

HONEYSUCKLE
G
Cut 4

HONEYSUCKLE
F
Cut 4

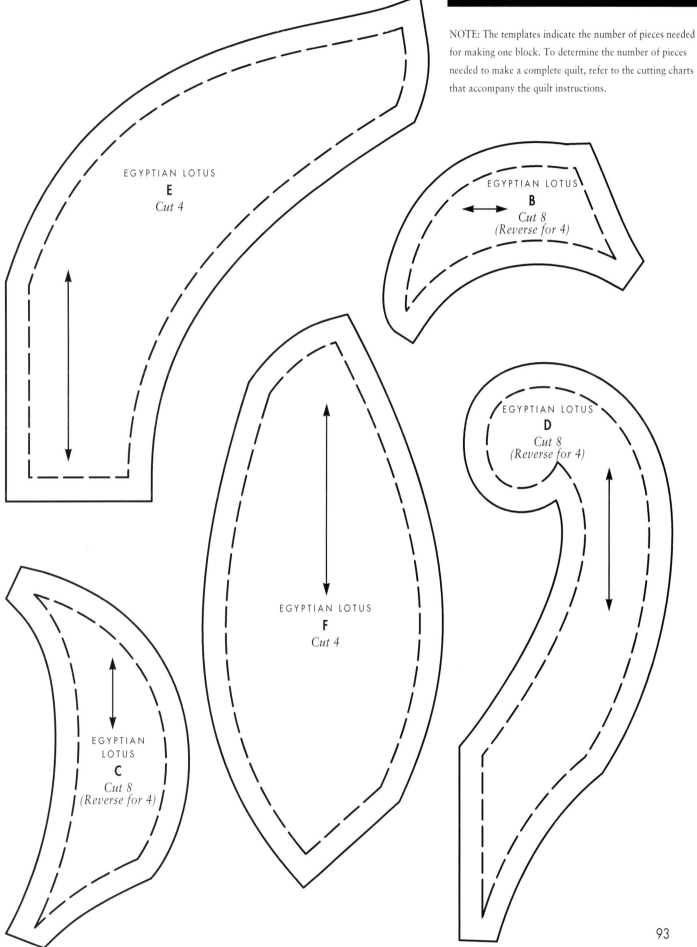

NOTE: The templates indicate the number of pieces needed for making one block. To determine the number of pieces needed to make a complete quilt, refer to the cutting charts that accompany the quilt instructions.

EGYPTIAN LOTUS
E
Cut 4

EGYPTIAN LOTUS
B
Cut 8
(Reverse for 4)

EGYPTIAN LOTUS
D
Cut 8
(Reverse for 4)

EGYPTIAN LOTUS
F
Cut 4

EGYPTIAN
LOTUS
C
Cut 8
(Reverse for 4)

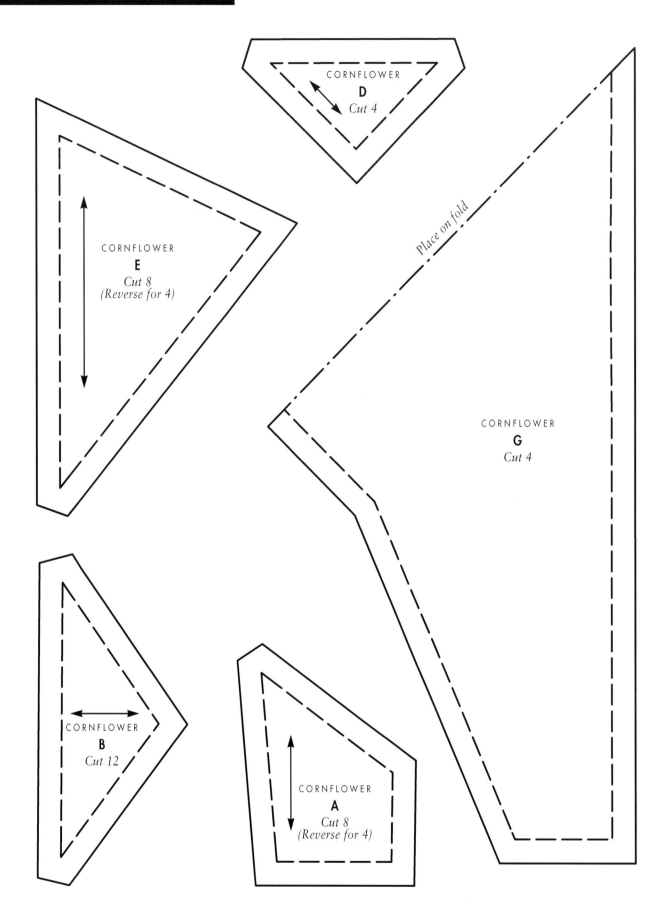

CORNFLOWER
D
Cut 4

CORNFLOWER
E
Cut 8
(Reverse for 4)

Place on fold

CORNFLOWER
G
Cut 4

CORNFLOWER
B
Cut 12

CORNFLOWER
A
Cut 8
(Reverse for 4)

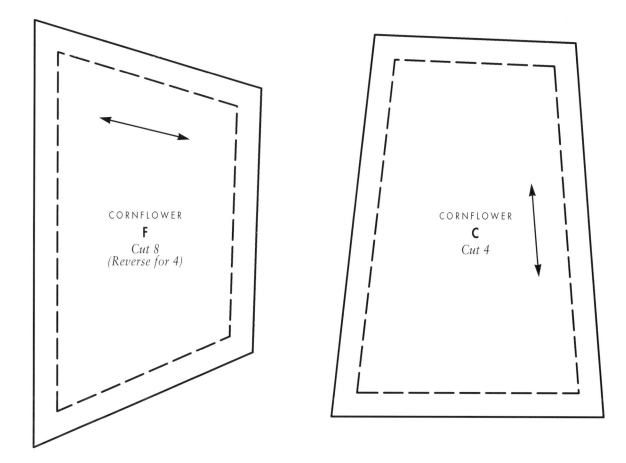

CORNFLOWER
F
Cut 8
(Reverse for 4)

CORNFLOWER
C
Cut 4

FLAME TREE

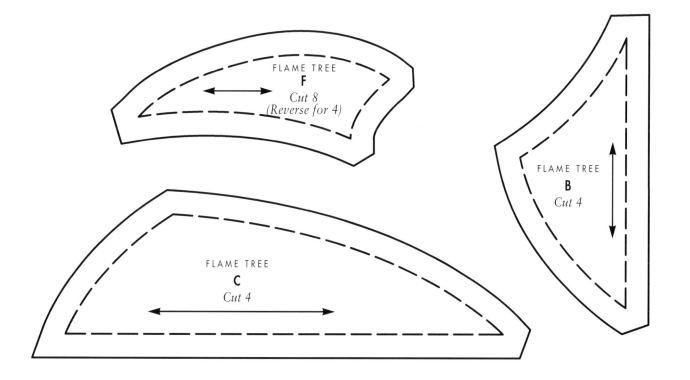

FLAME TREE
F
Cut 8
(Reverse for 4)

FLAME TREE
B
Cut 4

FLAME TREE
C
Cut 4

95

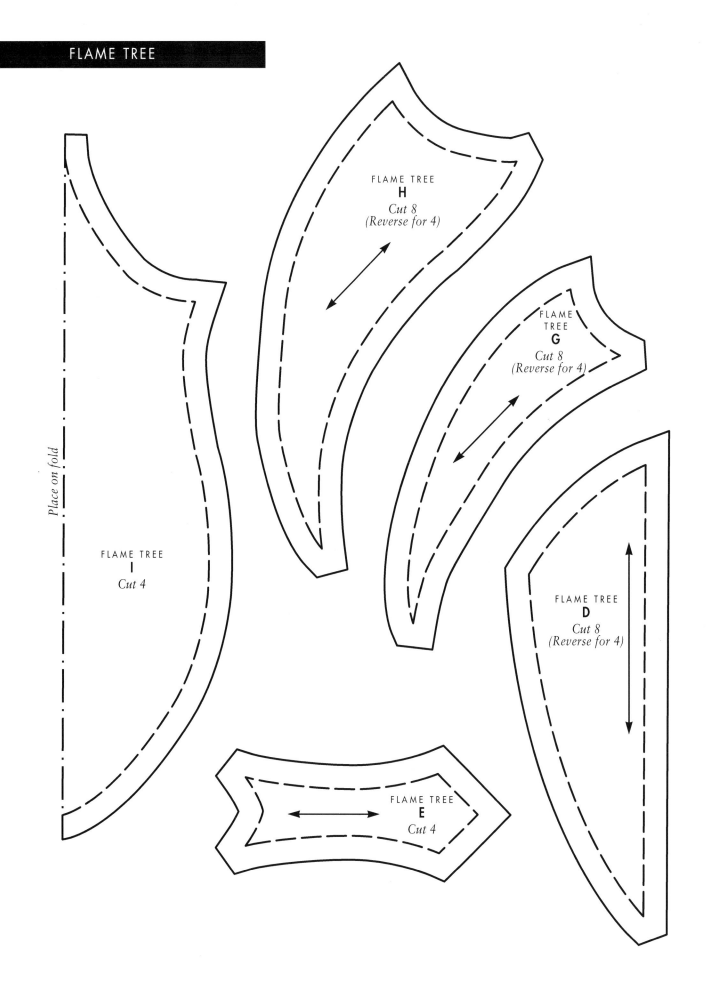

FLAME TREE
H
*Cut 8
(Reverse for 4)*

FLAME
TREE
G
*Cut 8
(Reverse for 4)*

FLAME TREE
D
*Cut 8
(Reverse for 4)*

Place on fold

FLAME TREE
I
Cut 4

FLAME TREE
E
Cut 4

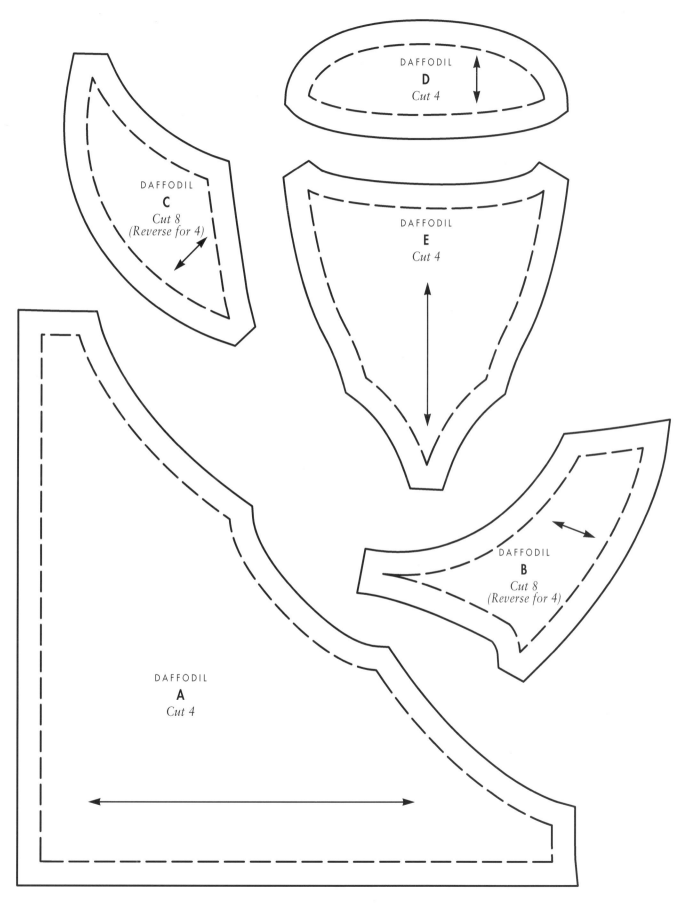

DAFFODIL
D
Cut 4

DAFFODIL
C
Cut 8
(Reverse for 4)

DAFFODIL
E
Cut 4

DAFFODIL
B
Cut 8
(Reverse for 4)

DAFFODIL
A
Cut 4

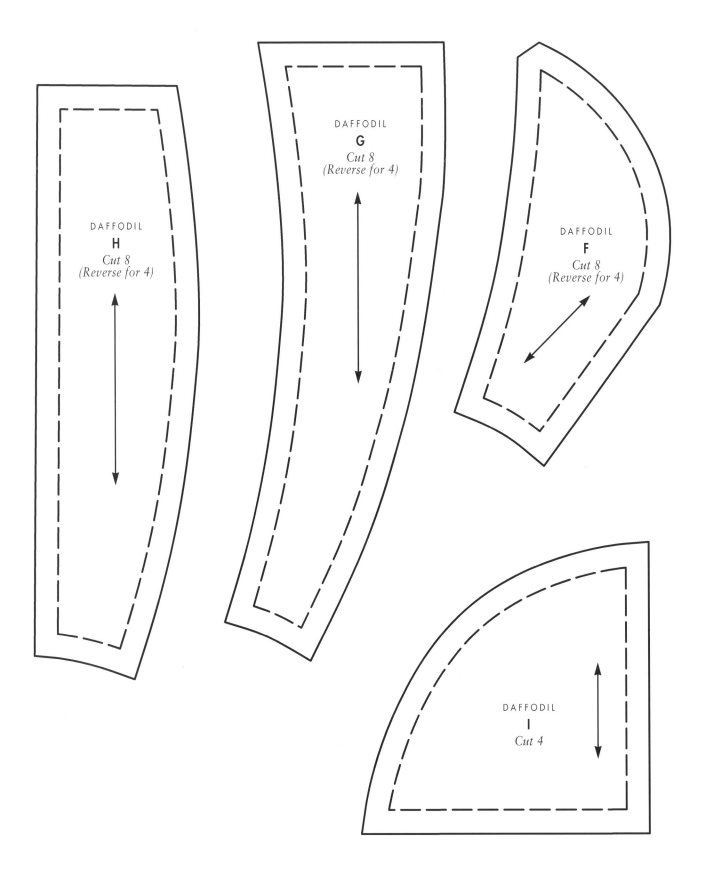

DAFFODIL
H
*Cut 8
(Reverse for 4)*

DAFFODIL
G
*Cut 8
(Reverse for 4)*

DAFFODIL
F
*Cut 8
(Reverse for 4)*

DAFFODIL
I
Cut 4

NOTE: The templates indicate the number of pieces needed for making one block. To determine the number of pieces needed to make a complete quilt, refer to the cutting charts that accompany the quilt instructions.

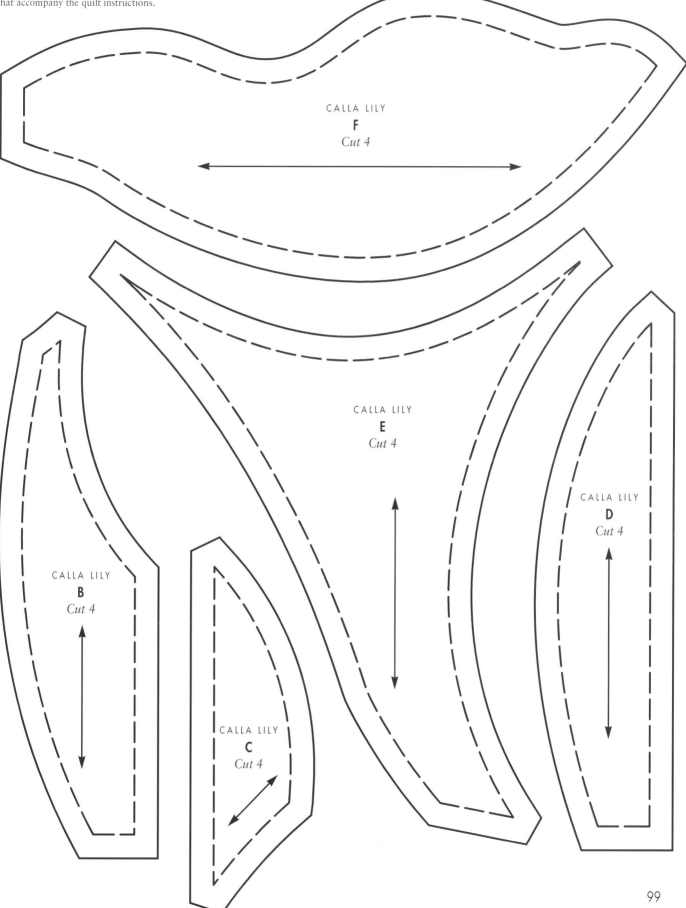

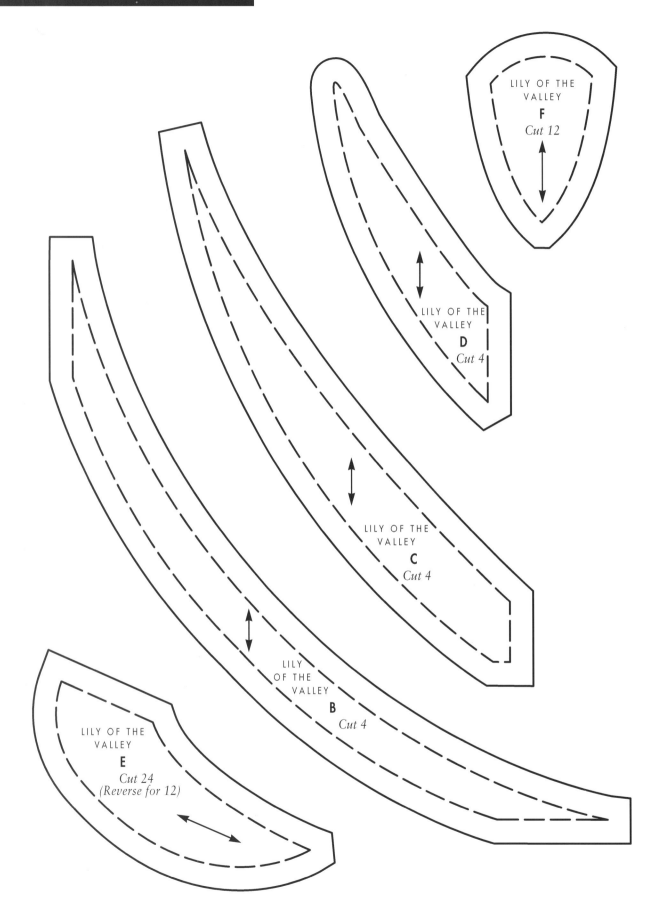

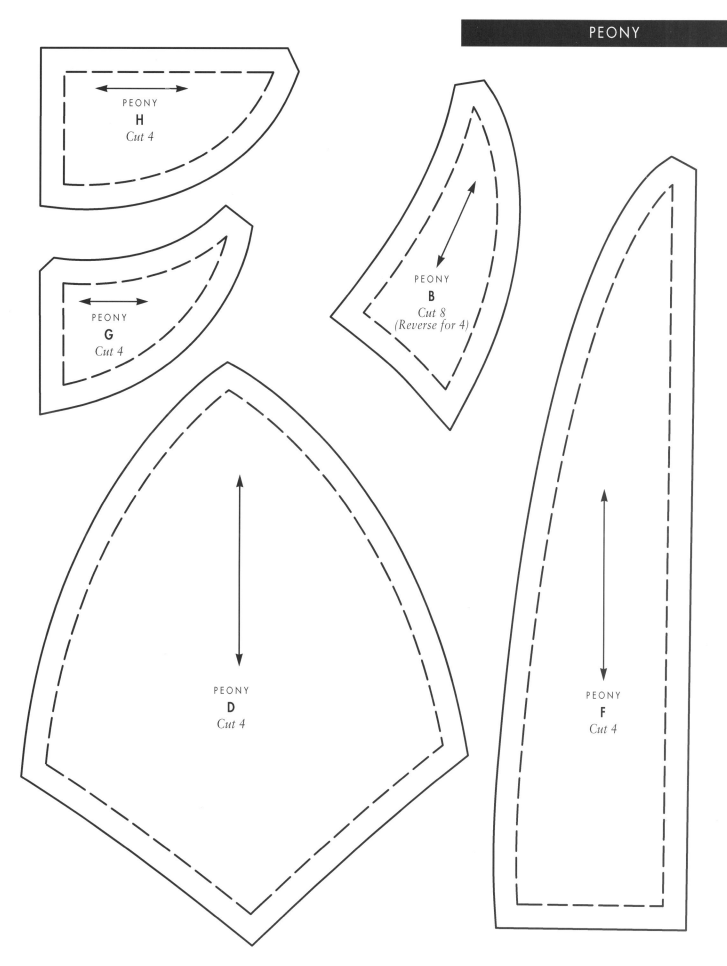

PEONY
H
Cut 4

PEONY
G
Cut 4

PEONY
B
Cut 8
(Reverse for 4)

PEONY
D
Cut 4

PEONY
F
Cut 4

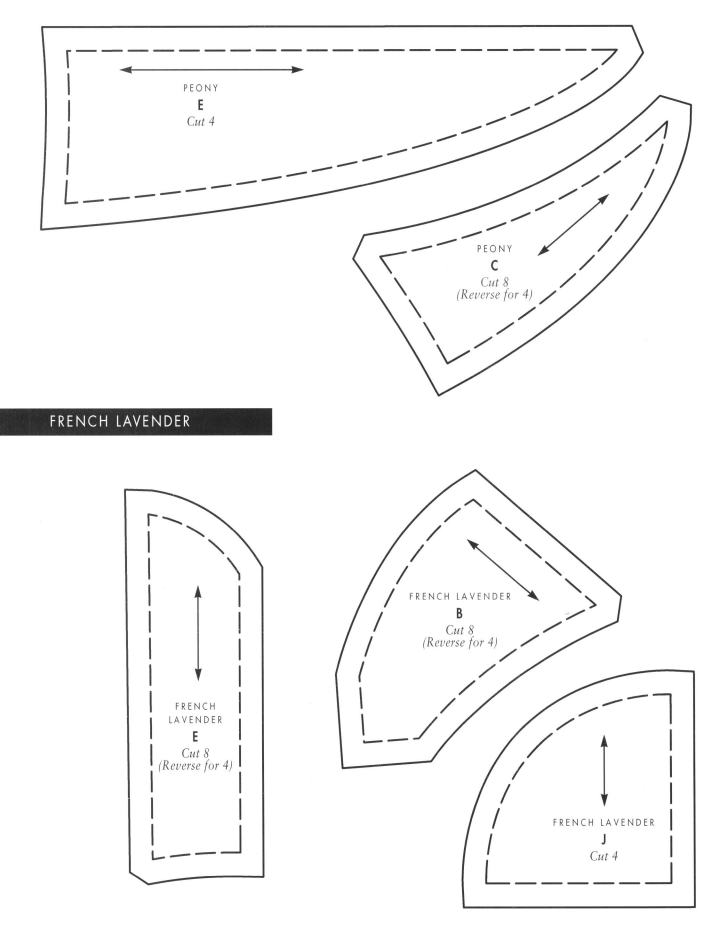

PEONY
E
Cut 4

PEONY
C
Cut 8
(Reverse for 4)

FRENCH LAVENDER

FRENCH
LAVENDER
E
Cut 8
(Reverse for 4)

FRENCH LAVENDER
B
Cut 8
(Reverse for 4)

FRENCH LAVENDER
J
Cut 4

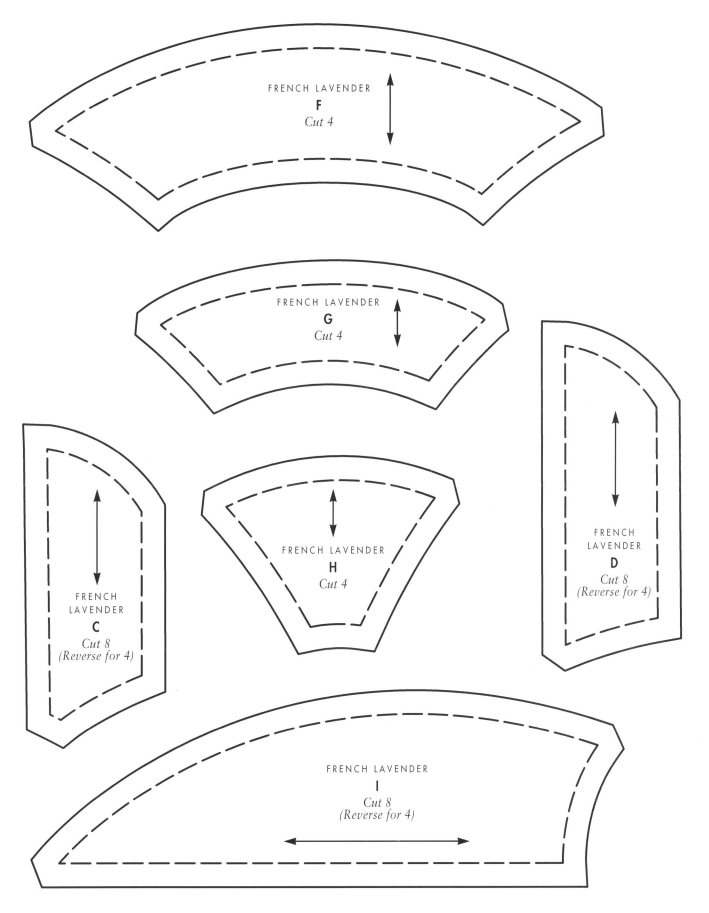

FRENCH LAVENDER
F
Cut 4

FRENCH LAVENDER
G
Cut 4

FRENCH
LAVENDER
D
Cut 8
(Reverse for 4)

FRENCH LAVENDER
H
Cut 4

FRENCH
LAVENDER
C
Cut 8
(Reverse for 4)

FRENCH LAVENDER
I
Cut 8
(Reverse for 4)

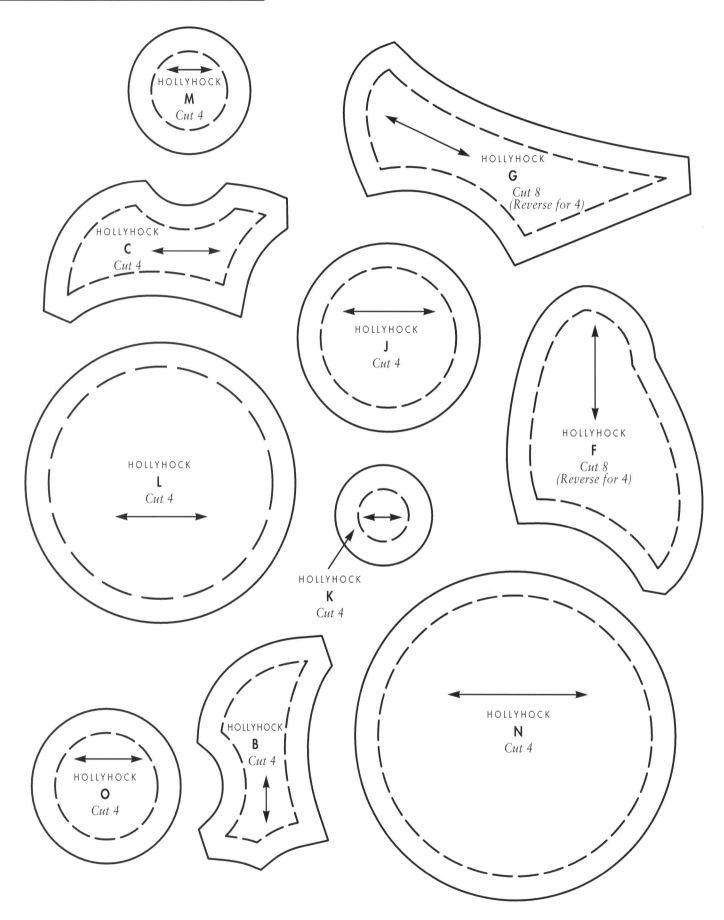

HOLLYHOCK
M
Cut 4

HOLLYHOCK
G
Cut 8
(Reverse for 4)

HOLLYHOCK
C
Cut 4

HOLLYHOCK
J
Cut 4

HOLLYHOCK
F
Cut 8
(Reverse for 4)

HOLLYHOCK
L
Cut 4

HOLLYHOCK
K
Cut 4

HOLLYHOCK
O
Cut 4

HOLLYHOCK
B
Cut 4

HOLLYHOCK
N
Cut 4

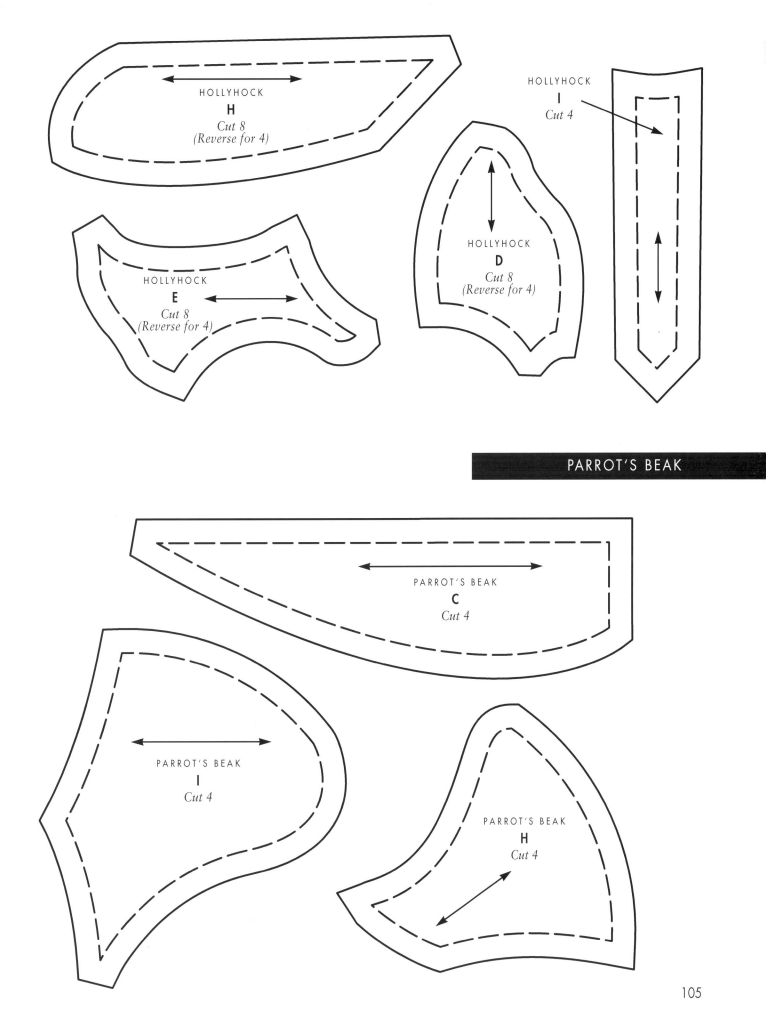

HOLLYHOCK
H
Cut 8
(Reverse for 4)

HOLLYHOCK
I
Cut 4

HOLLYHOCK
E
Cut 8
(Reverse for 4)

HOLLYHOCK
D
Cut 8
(Reverse for 4)

PARROT'S BEAK

PARROT'S BEAK
C
Cut 4

PARROT'S BEAK
I
Cut 4

PARROT'S BEAK
H
Cut 4

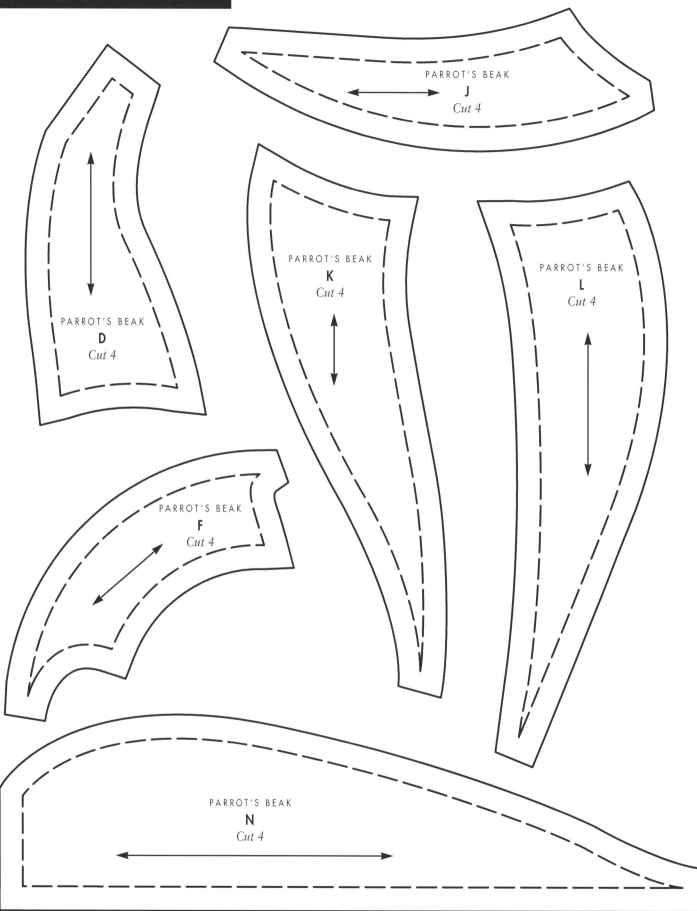

PARROT'S BEAK
J
Cut 4

PARROT'S BEAK
D
Cut 4

PARROT'S BEAK
K
Cut 4

PARROT'S BEAK
L
Cut 4

PARROT'S BEAK
F
Cut 4

PARROT'S BEAK
N
Cut 4

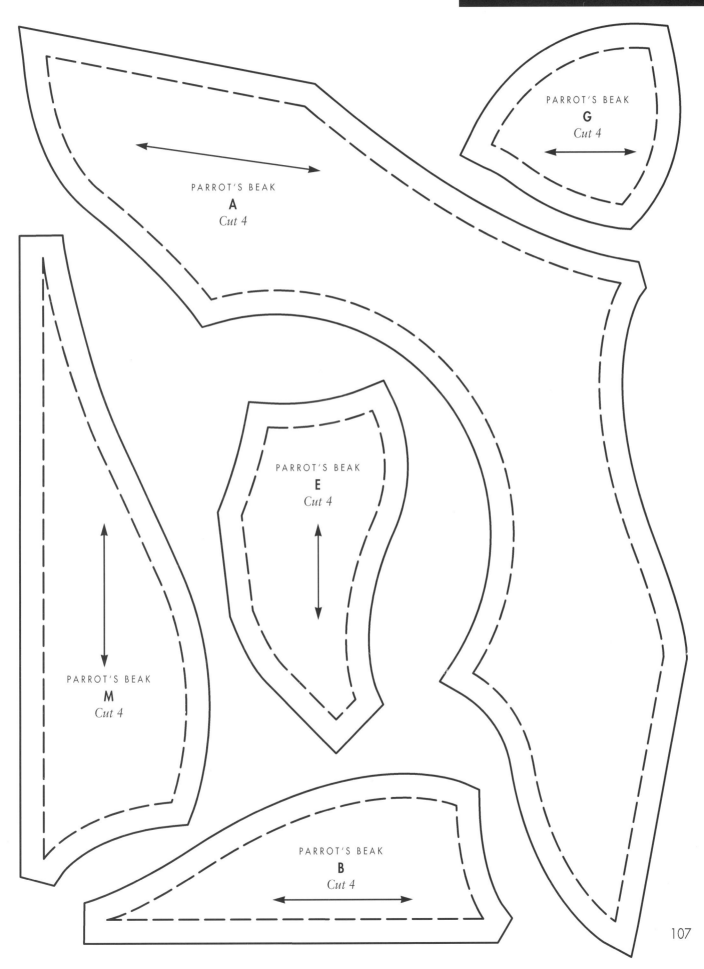

PARROT'S BEAK
G
Cut 4

PARROT'S BEAK
A
Cut 4

PARROT'S BEAK
E
Cut 4

PARROT'S BEAK
M
Cut 4

PARROT'S BEAK
B
Cut 4

107

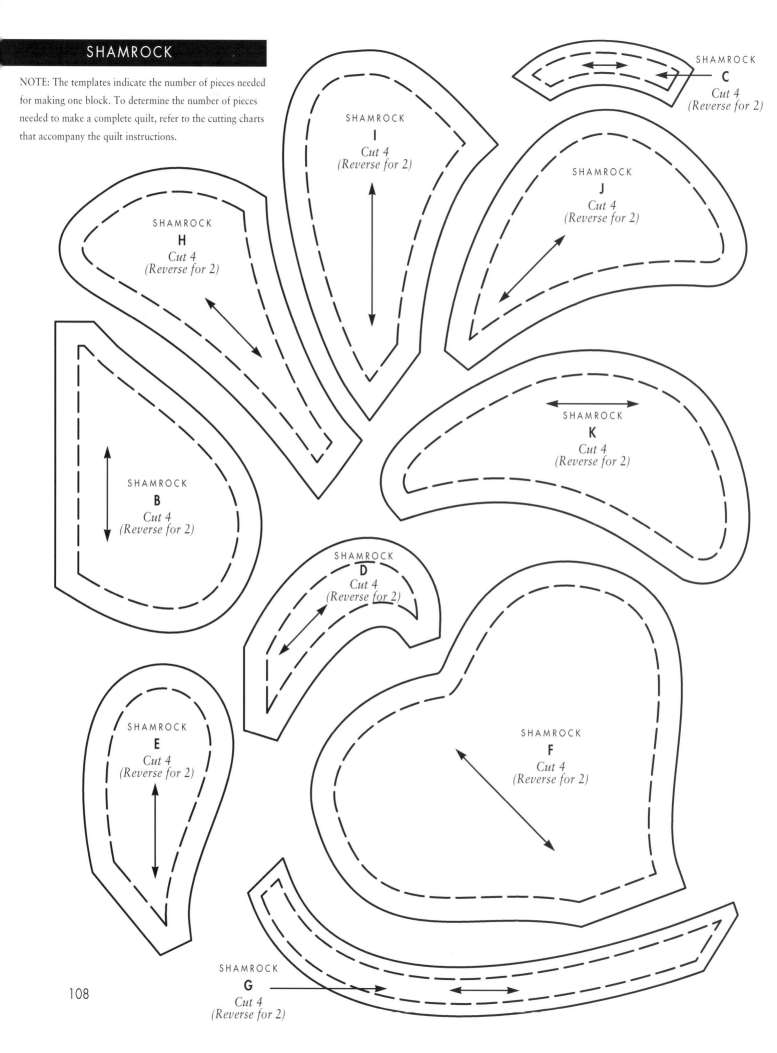

SHAMROCK

NOTE: The templates indicate the number of pieces needed for making one block. To determine the number of pieces needed to make a complete quilt, refer to the cutting charts that accompany the quilt instructions.

SHAMROCK
C
Cut 4
(Reverse for 2)

SHAMROCK
I
Cut 4
(Reverse for 2)

SHAMROCK
J
Cut 4
(Reverse for 2)

SHAMROCK
H
Cut 4
(Reverse for 2)

SHAMROCK
K
Cut 4
(Reverse for 2)

SHAMROCK
B
Cut 4
(Reverse for 2)

SHAMROCK
D
Cut 4
(Reverse for 2)

SHAMROCK
E
Cut 4
(Reverse for 2)

SHAMROCK
F
Cut 4
(Reverse for 2)

SHAMROCK
G
Cut 4
(Reverse for 2)

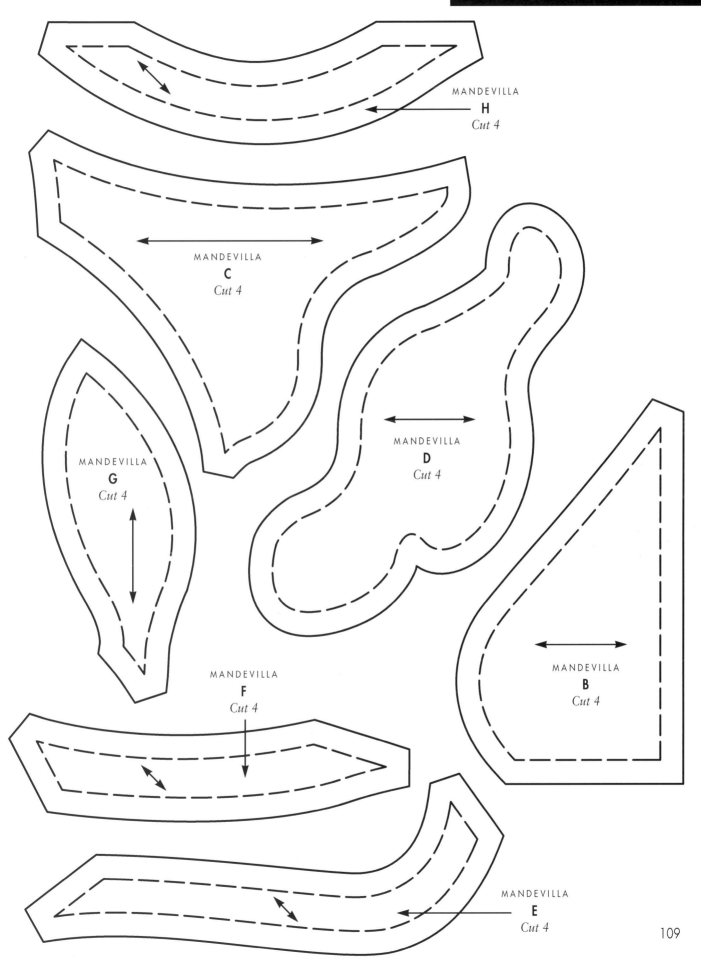

MANDEVILLA
H
Cut 4

MANDEVILLA
C
Cut 4

MANDEVILLA
D
Cut 4

MANDEVILLA
G
Cut 4

MANDEVILLA
B
Cut 4

MANDEVILLA
F
Cut 4

MANDEVILLA
E
Cut 4

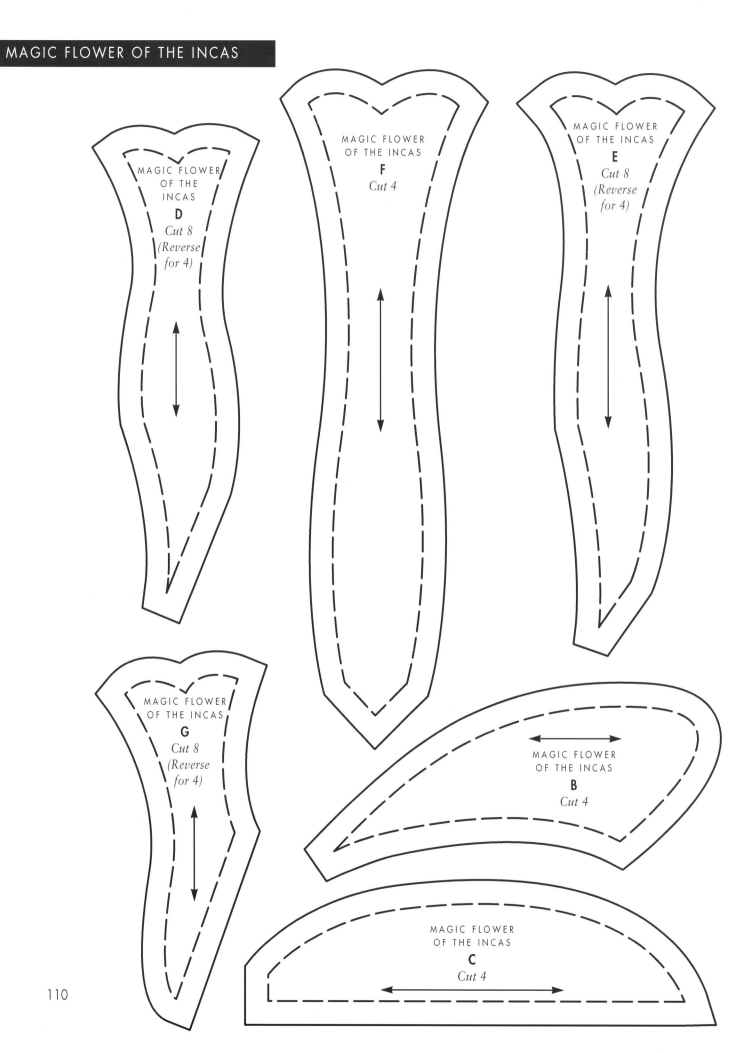

MAGIC FLOWER
OF THE
INCAS

D

*Cut 8
(Reverse
for 4)*

MAGIC FLOWER
OF THE INCAS

F

Cut 4

MAGIC FLOWER
OF THE INCAS

E

*Cut 8
(Reverse
for 4)*

MAGIC FLOWER
OF THE INCAS

G

*Cut 8
(Reverse
for 4)*

MAGIC FLOWER
OF THE INCAS

B

Cut 4

MAGIC FLOWER
OF THE INCAS

C

Cut 4

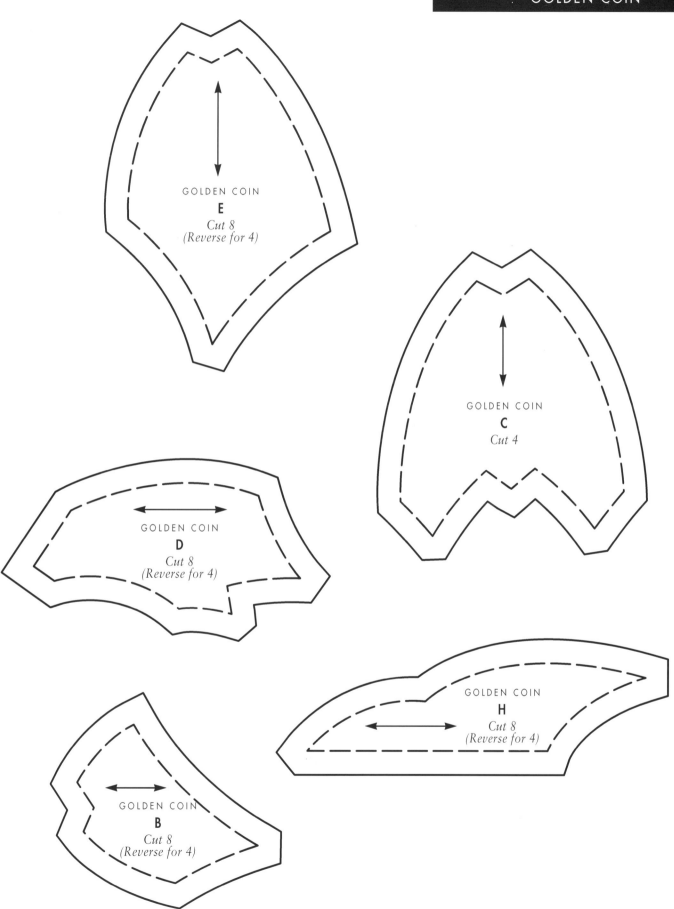

GOLDEN COIN
E
Cut 8
(Reverse for 4)

GOLDEN COIN
C
Cut 4

GOLDEN COIN
D
Cut 8
(Reverse for 4)

GOLDEN COIN
H
Cut 8
(Reverse for 4)

GOLDEN COIN
B
Cut 8
(Reverse for 4)

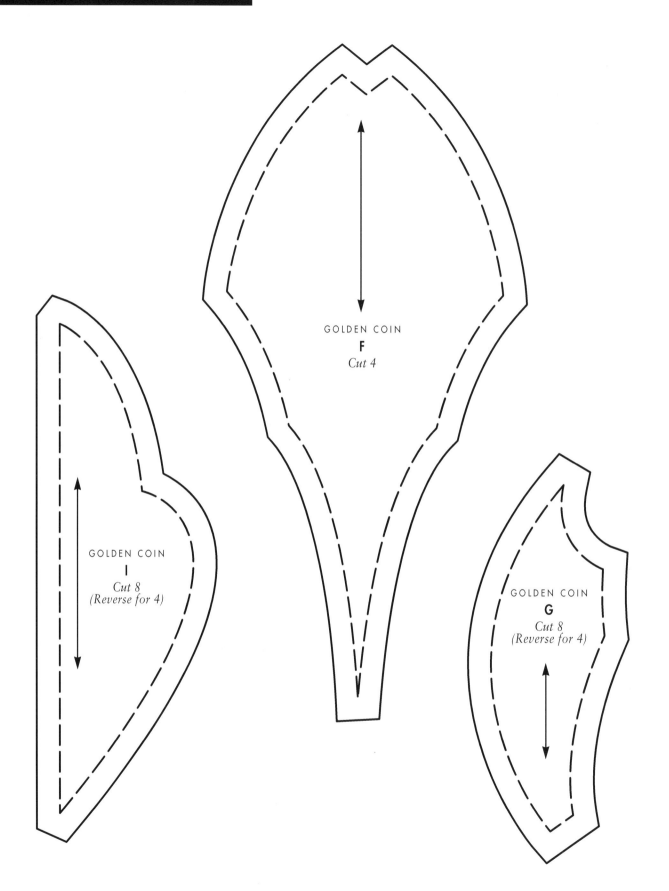

GOLDEN COIN
F
Cut 4

GOLDEN COIN
I
Cut 8
(Reverse for 4)

GOLDEN COIN
G
Cut 8
(Reverse for 4)

NOTE: The templates indicate the number of pieces needed for making one block. To determine the number of pieces needed to make a complete quilt, refer to the cutting charts that accompany the quilt instructions.

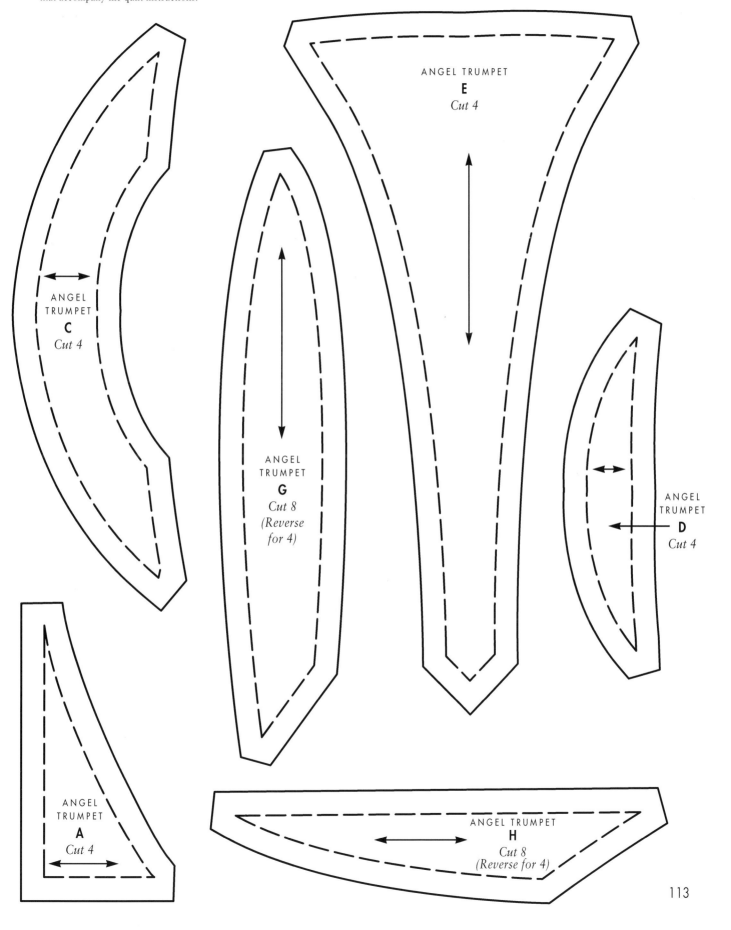

ANGEL TRUMPET
E
Cut 4

ANGEL
TRUMPET
C
Cut 4

ANGEL
TRUMPET
G
Cut 8
(Reverse
for 4)

ANGEL
TRUMPET
D
Cut 4

ANGEL
TRUMPET
A
Cut 4

ANGEL TRUMPET
H
Cut 8
(Reverse for 4)

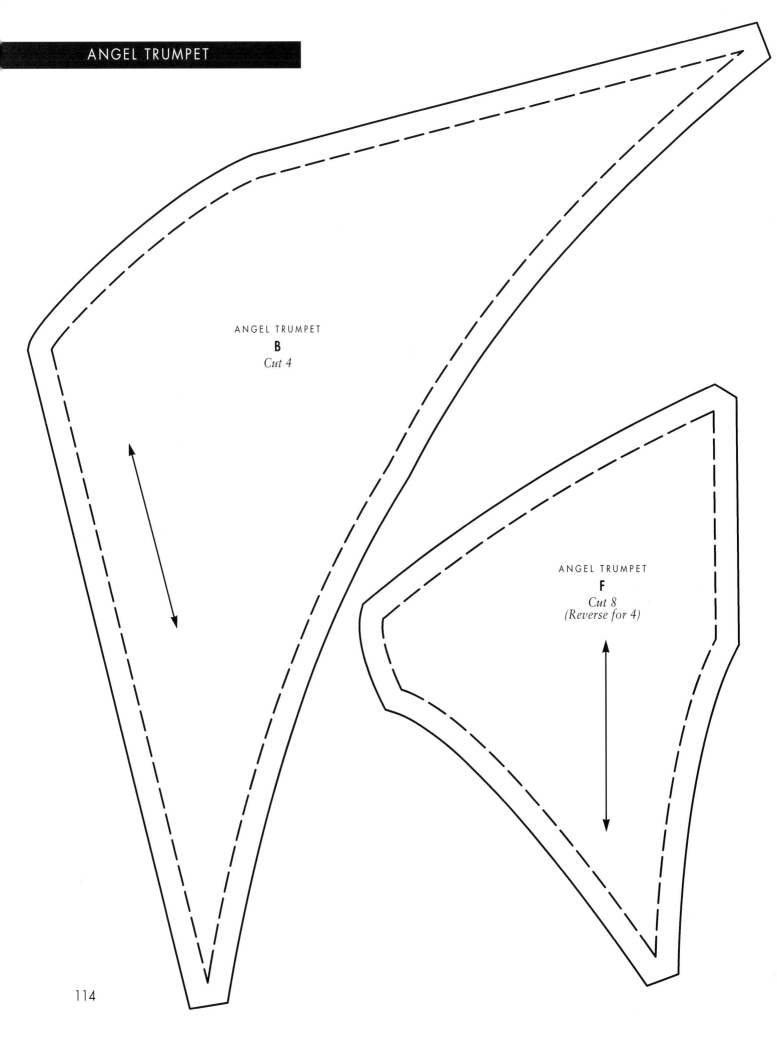

ANGEL TRUMPET
B
Cut 4

ANGEL TRUMPET
F
Cut 8
(Reverse for 4)

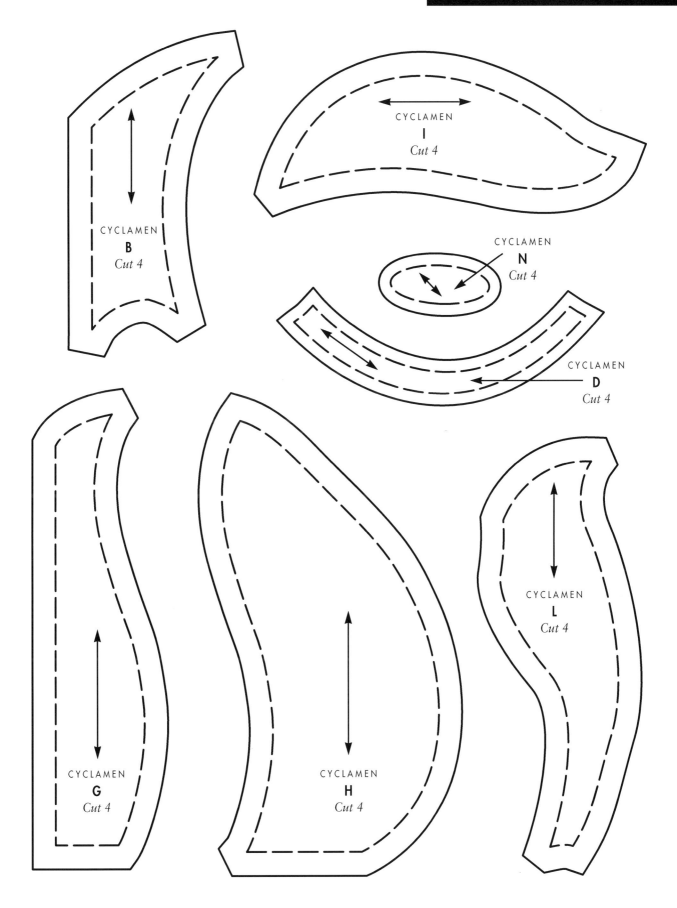

CYCLAMEN
I
Cut 4

CYCLAMEN
B
Cut 4

CYCLAMEN
N
Cut 4

CYCLAMEN
D
Cut 4

CYCLAMEN
L
Cut 4

CYCLAMEN
G
Cut 4

CYCLAMEN
H
Cut 4

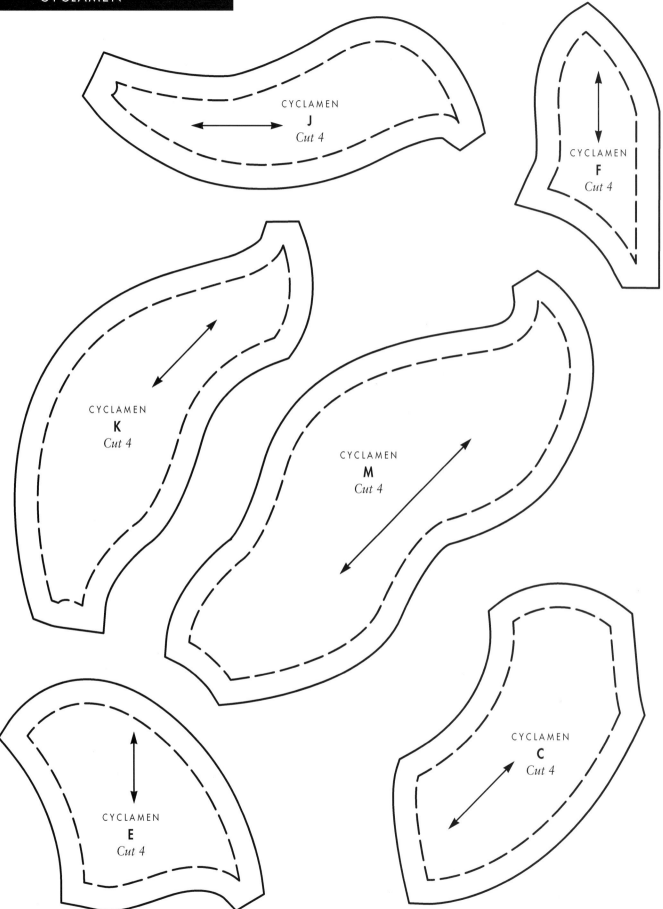

CYCLAMEN
J
Cut 4

CYCLAMEN
F
Cut 4

CYCLAMEN
K
Cut 4

CYCLAMEN
M
Cut 4

CYCLAMEN
E
Cut 4

CYCLAMEN
C
Cut 4

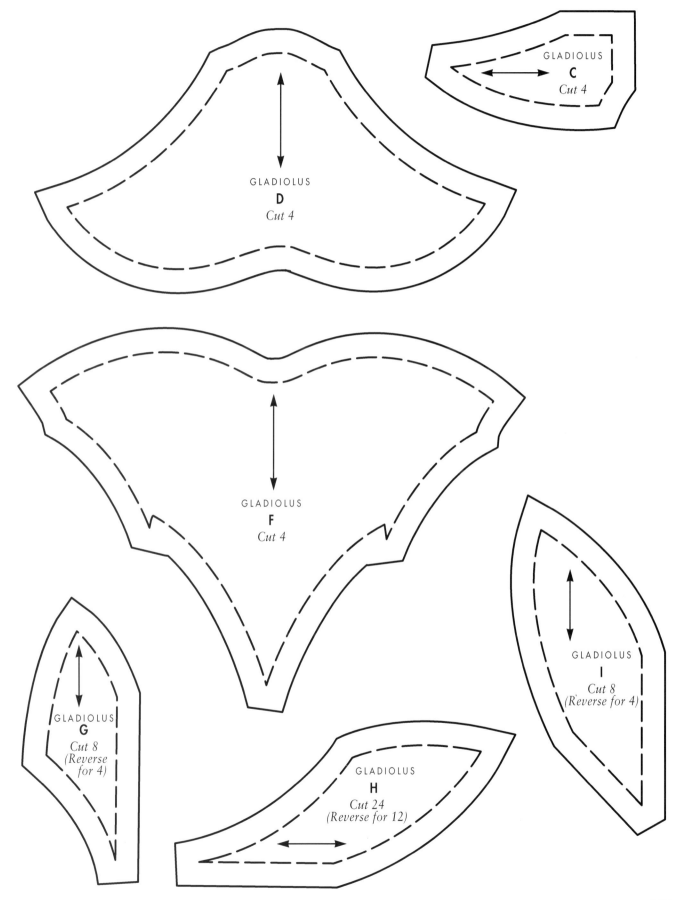

GLADIOLUS
C
Cut 4

GLADIOLUS
D
Cut 4

GLADIOLUS
F
Cut 4

GLADIOLUS
I
Cut 8
(Reverse for 4)

GLADIOLUS
G
Cut 8
(Reverse for 4)

GLADIOLUS
H
Cut 24
(Reverse for 12)

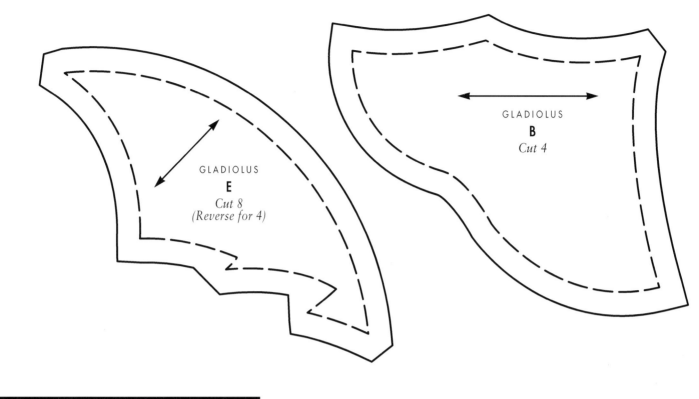

GLADIOLUS
E
Cut 8
(Reverse for 4)

GLADIOLUS
B
Cut 4

ROSE

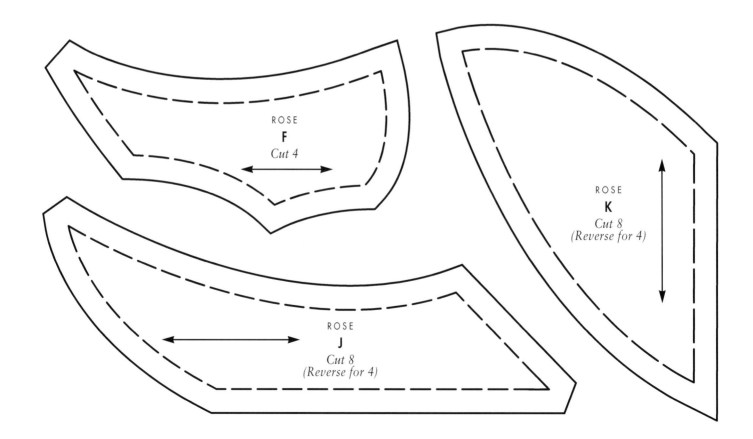

ROSE
F
Cut 4

ROSE
K
Cut 8
(Reverse for 4)

ROSE
J
Cut 8
(Reverse for 4)

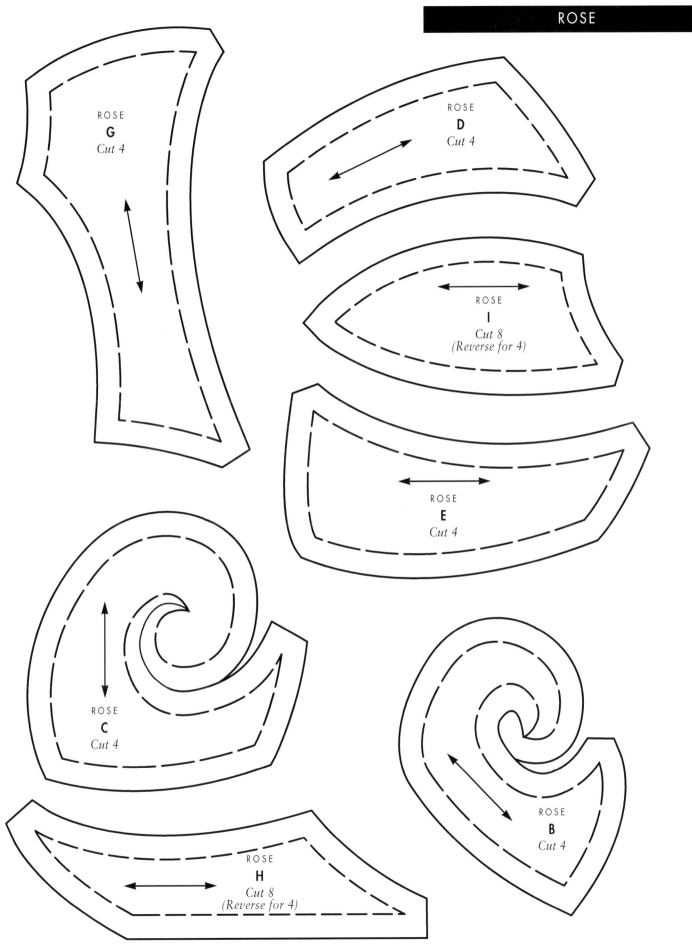

ROSE
G
Cut 4

ROSE
D
Cut 4

ROSE
I
Cut 8
(Reverse for 4)

ROSE
E
Cut 4

ROSE
C
Cut 4

ROSE
B
Cut 4

ROSE
H
Cut 8
(Reverse for 4)

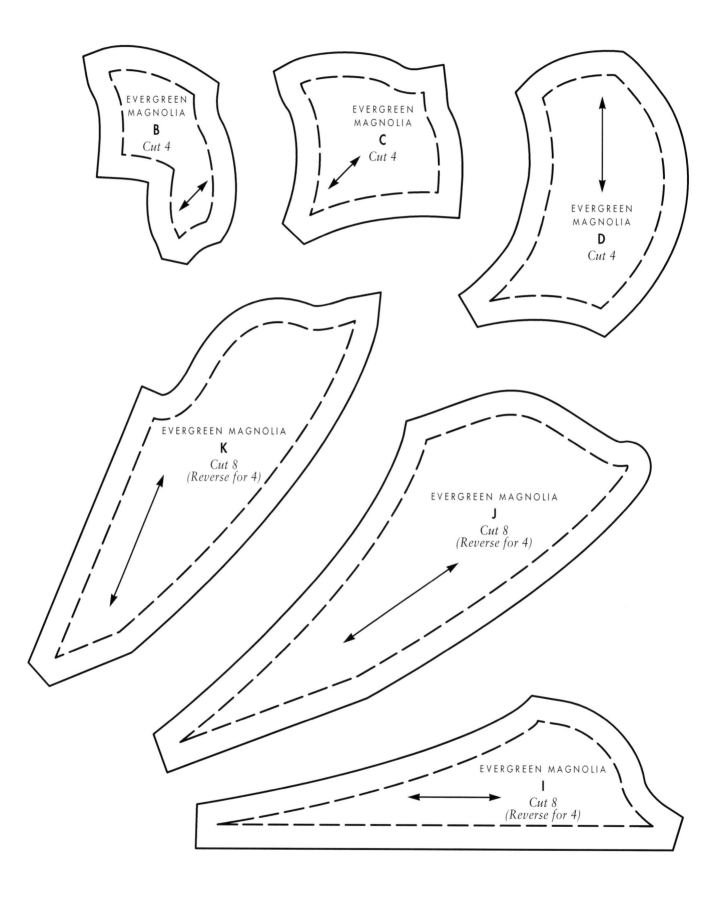

EVERGREEN
MAGNOLIA
B
Cut 4

EVERGREEN
MAGNOLIA
C
Cut 4

EVERGREEN
MAGNOLIA
D
Cut 4

EVERGREEN MAGNOLIA
K
Cut 8
(Reverse for 4)

EVERGREEN MAGNOLIA
J
Cut 8
(Reverse for 4)

EVERGREEN MAGNOLIA
I
Cut 8
(Reverse for 4)

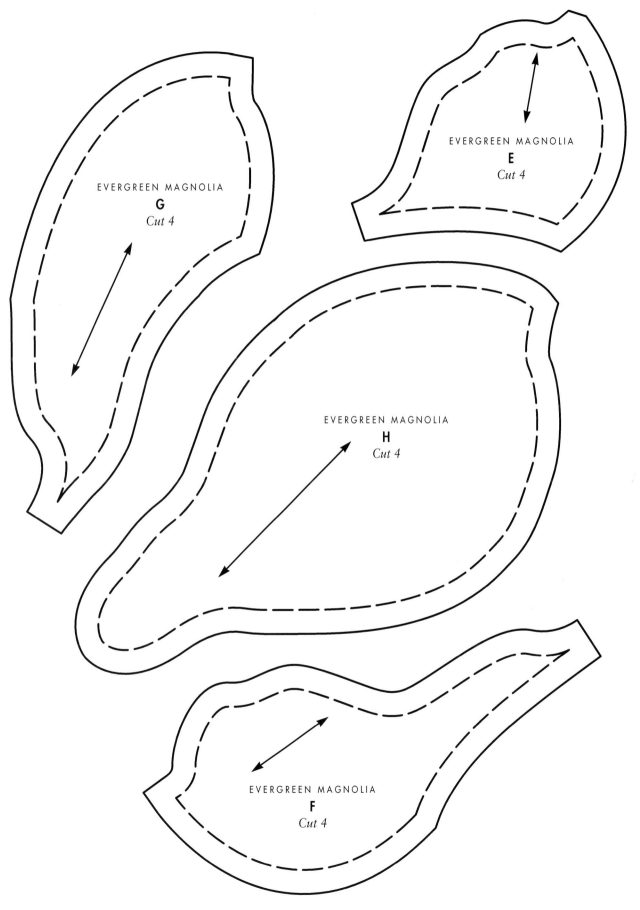

EVERGREEN MAGNOLIA
E
Cut 4

EVERGREEN MAGNOLIA
G
Cut 4

EVERGREEN MAGNOLIA
H
Cut 4

EVERGREEN MAGNOLIA
F
Cut 4

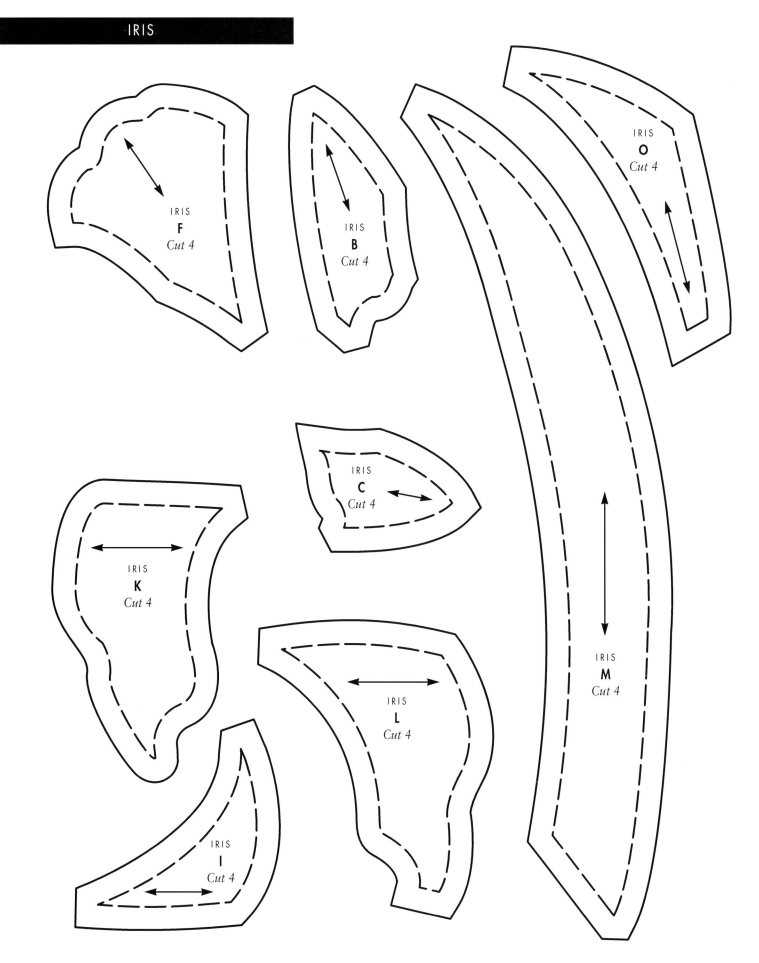

IRIS
F
Cut 4

IRIS
B
Cut 4

IRIS
○
Cut 4

IRIS
C
Cut 4

IRIS
K
Cut 4

IRIS
L
Cut 4

IRIS
M
Cut 4

IRIS
I
Cut 4

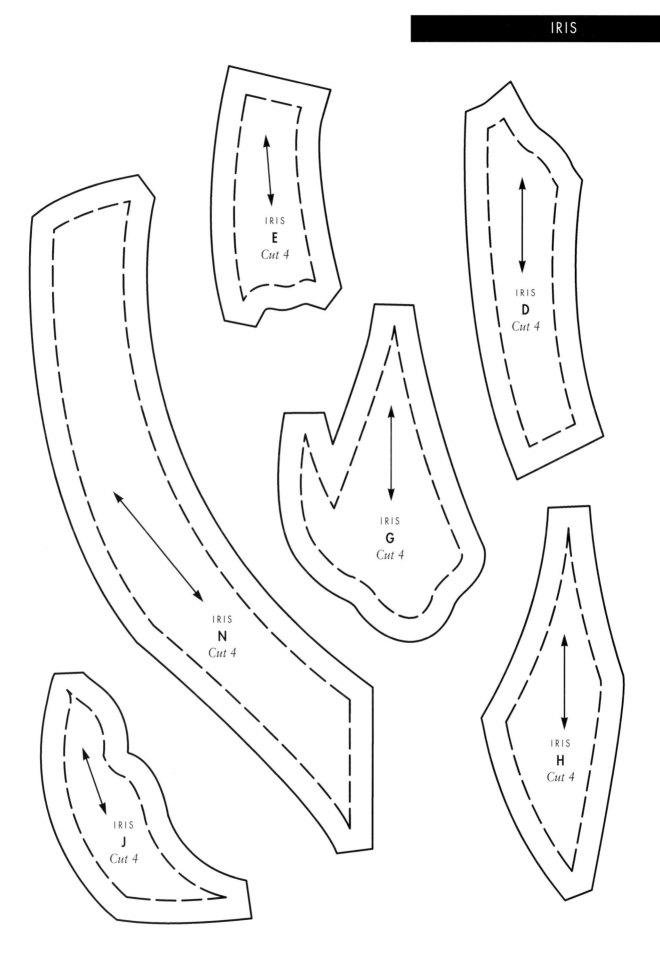

IRIS
E
Cut 4

IRIS
D
Cut 4

IRIS
G
Cut 4

IRIS
N
Cut 4

IRIS
H
Cut 4

IRIS
J
Cut 4

NOTE: The templates indicate the number of pieces needed for making one block. To determine the number of pieces needed to make a complete quilt, refer to the cutting charts that accompany the quilt instructions.

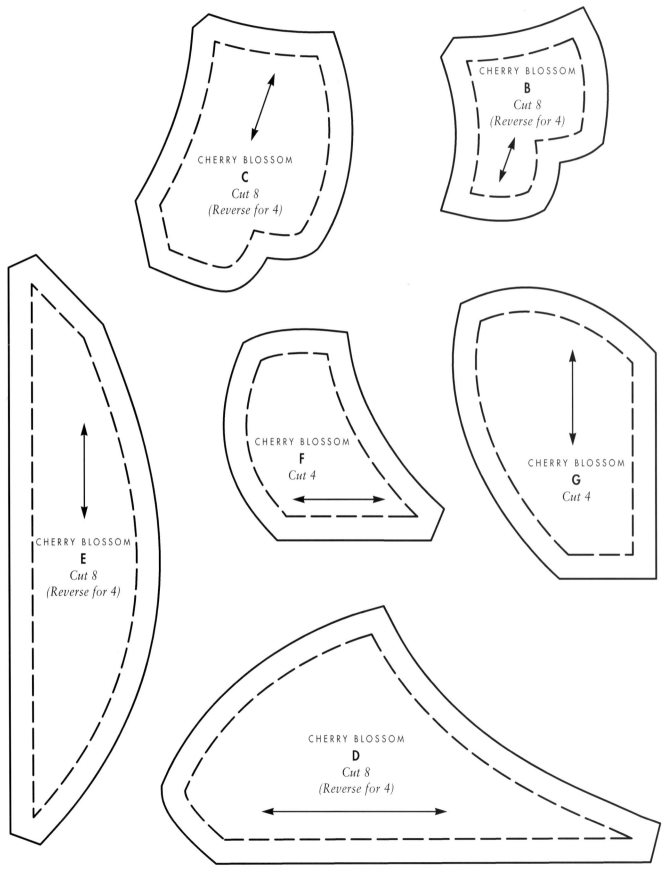

CHERRY BLOSSOM
C
Cut 8
(Reverse for 4)

CHERRY BLOSSOM
B
Cut 8
(Reverse for 4)

CHERRY BLOSSOM
E
Cut 8
(Reverse for 4)

CHERRY BLOSSOM
F
Cut 4

CHERRY BLOSSOM
G
Cut 4

CHERRY BLOSSOM
D
Cut 8
(Reverse for 4)

LESSON

PLANS

LESSON PLANS

Suggestions for a One-Day Workshop
Making a Simple Block: Peony

(FOR BEGINNING AND INTERMEDIATE QUILTERS)

During this sample lesson, students will make one of the easier blocks in this book. The process includes learning and practicing a precise method of hand piecing and looking at color and pattern in fabrics in a new way.

FIRST HOUR: Give each student one or more photocopies of the diagram for the *Peony* block (page 49). Discuss color selection and placement in the block: contrast of light and dark colors, texture, movement, and use of bold fabrics with large designs. Instruct students to experiment with colors by coloring their diagrams and then making their final decision as to the colors they will use.

SECOND HOUR: Students draw the placement patterns for the block on white paper, label each piece, and cut out each one (these do not include seam allowance). Students then make templates for the block (these do include seam allowance).

THIRD HOUR: After discussing the type of fabric to be used for the project, students select the fabrics that they will need to match their color sketches as closely as possible. They cut the fabric pieces using the templates, following the lengthwise grain or the print of the fabric patterns.

SUPPLY LIST FOR
EACH WORKSHOP

Sewing and quilting needles
Sewing and quilting thread
Straight pins
Paper and fabric scissors
Tracing paper
Template plastic
Ruler
Pencil
Colored pencils
Thimble
Fabric marker (or pencil)
White drawing paper
Notebook
Fabric for piecing the quilt top
Backing fabric
Batting

FOURTH AND FIFTH HOURS: Students lay the placement pattern pieces (without seam allowance) on the fabric pieces and draw around the edges with a fabric marker or pencil, indicating the seamlines. They pin and appliqué the pieces and iron them flat. Have them check, using the placement pattern pieces, that each appliquéd fabric piece is the correct size before going on to the next piece.

SIXTH HOUR: After completing the block top following the instructions and diagrams on page 49, students join the top, batting, and quilt backing with basting stitches. Students may quilt in freeform designs or following the seamlines.

Suggestions for an Extended Classroom Schedule
Making a More Complex Design:
Egyptian Lotus Block or Quilt

(FOR INTERMEDIATE AND ADVANCED QUILTERS)

These are ideas to be incorporated into a course for teaching experienced quilters how to refine their piecing, quilting, and appliqué skills. The course is based on a design that includes many curved seams, which are more difficult than straight seams but which offer more design possibilities. It also includes suggestions for those who wish to encourage students to create their own flower-based designs. Feel free to use these ideas along with your own teaching experience to modify the course as you wish.

Using the *Egyptian Lotus* design on page 35, begin by instructing students to make the block following the procedure outlined in the earlier lesson. (Students may make and finish one block or a complete quilt.)

During the piecing stage, demonstrate the type of appliqué technique used in this design; you may want to demonstrate other techniques for piecing curved seams and other forms of appliqué as well.

Discuss the use of color in the project — the colors in the *Egyptian Lotus* quilt shown in this book are very brilliant, and to get a similar feeling, students should choose fabrics in summer patterns with bright and bold prints.

To encourage creativity, demonstrate how new flower petal designs can be drawn. Students who have completed the *Egyptian Lotus* block shown in this book may wish to progress toward creating their own designs. Instruct students to make freehand drawings and fill in the areas using colored pencils.

Students who have created new designs can form small groups and share their ideas concerning new designs and patterns. In addition, you can conduct an open discussion with students about the pros and cons of each design.